GUNNER AND LAND GIRL

BOB AND CONNIE
THEIR WAR YEARS.

1939-1945

by

Steve Orwin

Strategic Book Group

Strategic Book Group

P.O. Box 333
Durham CT 06422

www.StrategicBookClub.com

ISBN: 978-1-60976-250-6

Contents

Part Two, Bob's story; The Gunner.

Introduction by their son Steve.

Today was bright and windy as I walked the beach and cliff-tops where I played as a child, as had my father thirty years before me. Now that my own children are young adults facing life's challenges, I can't help but reflect on how different their lives are from those of my parents at similar ages during the war.

Bob and Connie met at work, in a shipyard on the Tyne. My Dad worked in an office where Mother was a switchboard operator. They were eighteen and sixteen years old when they met and started walking to work together. Mother said it just happened that they coincided; sometimes she'd be walking along and would turn around to see a boy who looked like he'd just stopped running and sometimes she would be the one catching up. Then, somehow they started leaving work together for the walk home; and eventually my Dad would call round for her later in the evening after he'd finished his homework, as he was also studying at the time. They'd go for half an hour's walk together, though what a young man would want to take a girl out for a walk in the evening for, her mother just couldn't understand. They got to know each other well enough in the eighteen months before war started, to stay together through the uncertainties and separation, eventually marrying whilst Dad was on leave before his de-mob. They'd arranged this by mail whilst apart and Mother was waiting at the Church, not having seen her husband to be for four months, who arrived in the nick of time having travelled some 300 miles by train.

They were just embarking upon their adult lives when the Second World War began, dramatically changing their expectations and experiences. This is their story, or rather how two stories became one despite the intervening six years of danger and hardship.

My mother joined the Land Army and worked hard on a farm in the North East of England, whilst Dad went to France with the Royal Artillery, was evacuated from Dunkirk, then spent the rest of his war as a gunner on merchant shipping which took him round the world; and into some tight spots.

Bob and Connie survived together for sixty four years of marriage after the war, bringing up their family of three, and caring for each other. Sadly Bob died in April 2010 age 90.

They both missed their former ways of life once they returned to the industrial North East of England. Mum pined for the countryside and Dad missed the sea, but once the excitement was over, they just wanted to get on with having an ordinary life together. Whilst their story is very special for me, they are ordinary people and their tale is only one of what must be thousands of others that could have been told, so to this extent it is representative of a generation.

Mum's account is a series of observations and comments about life in and around a Dale farm, whilst Dad's is a more historical account of his career during the war. They both provide insight into private lives during public events, in a simple yet enigmatic way.

There are two individual books here, it would be nice to have had them side by side but practicalities dictate otherwise. So ladies first, we start with Connie's story.

I feel privileged to have had the opportunity of writing these memoirs and hope they offer you the reader, an opportunity for a personal glimpse into our collective past.

Steve Orwin.
September 2010.

PART ONE - THE LAND GIRL; CONNIE'S STORY.

Chapter one

First Signs of the Countryside.

I t was still dark as we walked through the village. Squat, gray stone houses edged the cobbled square with the war memorial, bus stop and blacksmiths. A small group of men stood around, silhouetted by the glow from the furnace. They stamped their feet and rubbed their hands, eyeing us as we made our way along the street, laughing and joking in their local dialect. We soon found they would be our workmates; and that the blacksmith's would become a familiar place to call.

I had just met Helen the day before, at the land Army hostel outside the village. Now in our dungarees, jumper, coat and stiff new boots, we were on our way to our first day's work.

I was eighteen when the war started and Bob my boyfriend, later husband, was twenty when he was called up. Because I missed him and wanted to do something to help, I joined the Land Army. So here I was, walking in the dark into an experience that left a lasting impression on my life.

A mile later, away from the shelter of the hills, we looked for our farm but could only find a barn and sawmill. The snow had soaked our legs and the wind bit through our clothes, as red nosed and shivering we approached some men, who paused to stare in amusement.

One asked "Ist tha land lasses?" His blue eyes twinkled in his ruddy face as he assessed our discomfort, "Best find you an indoor job," he said, leading us into the long, high barn, filled with 'chop,' a mixture of hay and straw for horse fodder.

We knew we were lucky to have shelter and our spirits rose as the work, filling hundredweight sacks, warmed us and dried our clothes. We looked out of the window at the fields covered in snow, the sun rising and sparkling in the tree tops, stroking the other side of the valley with its golden luster. This turned out to be one of the coldest Januarys of the war, but in youthful optimism we sang as we worked and talked of our town lives. Just two days ago Helen had worked in a factory and I'd been in an office.

Soon we felt hungry and looked at our lunch boxes. They were big and strong, but our dismay would be hard to imagine when we found their meager contents, thin sandwiches of paste and jam and a square of sponge cake. It was only 9:30 am and we were ravenous. Breakfast was a distant memory as we'd left the hostel at 7:00 am and our next meal wasn't due until 6:00 pm. We nibbled a little and resumed our work of filling sacks, in a quieter mood.

After another two hours we tried to straighten our aching backs. The shovels felt heavy in our blistered hands, there were straws and hayseeds in our hair and they itched under our clothes. We needed the toilet, but couldn't contemplate asking the men where to go; we guessed much of their laughter was already at our expense.

Noon came and Jack called to us, he said he'd take us to his home across the fields. We trudged across the ice to a terrace where he lived with his wife and family of five children. Though he'd worked all morning in sub-zero conditions he was warm and energetic. He introduced us proudly to his wife, a good humored and confident lady who welcomed us hospitably. Soon we were sat round a table by the fire with rounds of bread and fried eggs on our plates. The laughing chattering children, faces glowing in the warmth of the fire, were a contrast to the cold of our morning's experience in the barn.

Jack was a 'hind' in charge of the horses. Some came to the stables for a rest after working in the forestry side of the business, others came for breaking in.

His 'Boss' lived with his family in the 'Home Farm' on the other side of the river. He was a rich man who drove a hard bargain and worked his men hard, but never asked them to do a job he wouldn't do himself. He'd had a hard life, which toughened him and sharpened his wits. Born illegitimately into poverty, he acquired a run-down horse and did odd jobs. When the horse's condition improved, he sold it and bought another and so his business progressed to include land, forestry, sawmills, quarries and aggregates. He watched his workers through binoculars and sacked those who didn't come up to expectations. He was respected, but I hoped I wouldn't meet him for a long time.

The lunch hour passed too rapidly and reluctantly we left, but glad of the invitation to call again. Our spirits lifted, we enjoyed the challenge of the biting wind as we crossed the ice hard fields past a group of huddled sheep as we returned to work.

The filled sacks had been removed from the barn and a larger pile of empty ones replaced them. The considerable hole we'd carved in the 'chop' had been filled, so once more we rolled up our sleeves and started to shovel.

As time went on, we came to enjoy our morning walks through the village. Though early, it was always busy and we waved to the men at the blacksmiths and laughed at their wolf-whistles. Our hands roughened, and backs strengthened, but we got bored filling bags of chop. This wasn't what I'd thought I'd joined the Land Army for; then one day Jack said I was to go to the stables with him.

Chapter two

Horseflesh.

I'd expected rows of loose boxes, with horses' heads looking over to see who'd come in. I'd imagined they would whinny softly to Jack who fed and cared for them, but my illusions were shattered by two rows of huge buttocks. It was a windowless building with a central concrete path, flanked by lines of huge restless flanks and shuffling hooves. I followed Jack through the dimness to the far end of the building, dwarfed by those strong hindquarters and horribly conscious of the proximity of those hooves. I was shown the box of chop and oats. Jack measured an amount then slapped a horse on the rump. As it clip clopped to one side, he walked between it and the partition of the stall, to put its food in a manger. Jack told me that was what I had to do, then sweep up the muck into a barrow and dump it outside on the heap. He went to do some other jobs and said he'd be back soon.

It seemed simple, so with a measure of feed I approached the first horse and clapped it on the rump. It didn't move. I gave it another slap but still no response. "Move over" I said, but it was deaf. I tried squeezing through, but it shifted its bulk to block my way and leant on me. As I squeezed out fast, it stamped its hoof just missing my toes. The other horses sensed the situation and became restless too, their tails swished and heads strained against their halters. I didn't fancy my chances with any of them!

I thought of the milkman's horse back home, a sweet little thing that pulled the float that I'd ridden in as a child. With fresh determination I approached another horse and slapped it as hard as I dared. A horse further down the line lashed out with both feet, I'd never seen anything like that before, the speed was incredible. If I'd been behind it I would have been a skin-full of splinters. Somewhat shaken I appealed to the awkward monster, "Oh come along, do move over, I've got your food for you."

An unrestrained chuckle from the doorway surprised me, I turned to see a fat little man with a round face and a horseshoe embroidered down his shirt front and I guessed I had met 'The Boss'.

"T bloody hoss canna understand thee," he boomed, "Dey it like this." He walloped the rump and shouted "Git up yer great bugger," and the horse clip clopped to one side. "Dey it that way," he yelled at me. In his dynamic presence one had no choice but to obey. I whammed the horse and bellowed "Git up yer great bugger" with instant success.

He watched me feed three more horses then left, highly amused and chuckling gleefully. That was the worst swearword I'd used in my life.

I worked around the stables for a few more days, doing odd jobs, cleaning and taking the horses out to drink at the water tank. Most were large shire horses resting from their grueling work in the forests. They were not trusting or to be trusted, they would kick, bite and stamp. Jack's job, caring for them and doctoring them was dangerous and I was relieved when the next week I was told to report to the Home Farm.

Chapter three

Life in the Hostel.

Though we were in the heart of the countryside, it was only forty miles from where most of us lived on the industrial coast. So if we had money for our bus fares, there was just time to get home after our Saturday morning work and return to the hostel for Sunday evening.

I would usually go to see Jack's family on my way back from home and sit by the fire in their kitchen, watching the younger children getting washed in the tin bath. The fire heated an oven on one side and a boiler on the other, which was filled by the oldest girl carrying water in a jug from the kitchen tap. When it was hot, the water was drawn off from a tap near the base. After the baby was bathed and dried on a towel warmed on the oven, he was cuddled by one of us whilst the next youngest was bathed then handed to someone whilst the next was done. It was strange to see Jack who was so tough with the horses, gently nursing his children, their little arms wrapped around his neck and kissing his rough red cheeks.

After the children had gone to bed the rest of us had supper. This was a grand meal as Sunday was baking day. There was meat tart, prune pie, custard tart and delicious home-made bread. We relaxed, laughed and talked about the week and then Jack's wife would walk me back to the hostel, whatever the weather.

The hostel was a busy place on Sunday nights, girls came back in all sorts of moods some were glad to have seen their boyfriends, and some were home sick.

The building was L shaped, one arm was a dormitory with forty beds, the other, was the recreation and dining area, each was heated by a coke burning stove at each end.

The dormitory was partitioned; we slept in bunks, two pairs to each partition, with a wardrobe, chest of drawers and a mirror. The recreation area had some chairs around the stoves and there were long tables and chairs in the dining room.

The cook was a young lady from the village and our evening meals were plain but filling. Our lunch boxes weren't so good though, it was all right if we got cups of tea and something to eat from the farmers during the day, as otherwise the few meager sandwiches weren't enough to see us through.

The warden's rooms were beyond the kitchen, where she lived in luxury, with carpets, tasteful furnishings and curtains! How easy for such a privileged woman to be pleasant, it seemed to us too nice a job to be classed as war work.

The ablution area was at the end of the dormitory, with toilets, basins, baths, a sink for washing clothes and a large hand-wringer with wooden rollers. There was no hint of luxury in our part of the building, but we were glad to gather round the stoves for warmth on winter evenings, whilst those who had the energy could play table tennis.

In the summer we would lie on our bunks and read, or write letters to our boyfriends in the forces. We didn't argue much and were a hardworking lot. We elected a head girl each term to deal with ideas and complaints and mediate with the warden. There were never many complaints, for Britain was at war. Our loved ones were away fighting for us and our families at home lived with the fear of being bombed. Their nights were often spent in air raid shelters and there were shortages and rationing.

We knew that Britain needed every man and woman to do their utmost to help our armed forces and keep industry moving. Our work to increase food production was necessary to keep it all going.

Chapter four

The Home Farm Pigs.

To get to the Home Farm I crossed the bridge and climbed up a steep hill before turning into a long drive bordered by hedges, with rows of daffodils in the spring. The front of the house had long sloping gardens overlooking the river and the hillside beyond. There was a garden at the back too, where I saw a black Rolls Royce with a chauffeur to keep it polished.

As soon as I arrived, I was put to mucking out a byre that housed a small dairy herd. I had to wash the cows' udders, feed the cows and then carry milk to the dairy. The Boss's wife showed me how to clean and sterilize the dairy equipment. She worked quickly and efficiently and expected me to do the same.

When the dairy work was finished the hens had to be fed, then great buckets of swill carried to the pigs. They were treated to vegetable rubbish with fried eggs, lumps of bread and tea leaves. It was a long way to their field by the river, so by the time I got there, my arms felt as if they were pulled from their sockets. When I rested the buckets to open the gate, I heard a huge squeal as several pigs rushed towards me from their sty. I managed to slip through the gate and close it firmly before they reached it. What a rumpus they'd create if they got out, especially if they reached that immaculate Rolls Royce! To my horror, the largest, fattest pig had outrun the others and was advancing with hideous squeals. She smacked her head greedily into the bucket but I somehow slithered and staggered on through their pushing noses and the churned up mud, to reach the troughs and pour the swill in. I ached with relief when I finally reached them, feeling I'd faced an alien army. Why did the troughs have to be so far from the gate? I returned to the house and took the buckets back to the kitchen ready for refilling.

Chapter five

Clearing Stones.

When winter granted a temporary reprieve, I was sent to clear stones from a field so they wouldn't damage farm machinery in the spring. It was so relaxing to stand alone in the middle of the field, with no one to say 'do this and that' and with no charging pigs! The ground was a bit wet after the snow, but the air was fresh and the view splendid. I could see bare hedges and trees in the green fields below, whilst horses, carts and cars were driving along the road through the dale. I could see the sawmill and stables where Helen and I had first started work, a shepherd driving sheep with his dogs and smoke curling from the chimneys of many houses.

I threw the smaller stones to the walls and carried the larger ones. My back was getting strong with all the activity. I wondered where Helen was working now, the Boss never seemed to keep us together and I didn't see much of her in the hostel as she was very involved with a new boyfriend who lived locally. I learned later that she'd been sacked after her probationary period, leaving me as the only female in the large workforce.

Soon it was lunch-time and I went back to the farm to eat my sandwiches, along with a pint pot of tea offered to me by Mark, the Boss's eighteen year old son. I took it to the warm byre and found a milking stool to sit on, for an hour of comparative luxury.

When I went back to the field, Mark and his friend Eddy joined me. Conversation was a bit stilted as they were trying not to swear, they didn't know what to make of working with a town girl. An awful lot of stones got cleared that afternoon though, along with a few sly winks and jibes.

Chapter six

Rats and Cattle.

I was shown how to milk a cow the following day. Though interesting and potentially useful to know how to do this by hand, I knew it was unnecessary here in a byre which was well equipped with milking machines and water basins for each cow. It was funny how many people were just 'passing through' and lingered to watch as the cow neatly kicked me, the milking stool and the bucket into the gutter. Naturally it caused much amusement, though the audience melted away as I picked myself up, determined to try again.

By lunchtime I felt I'd had enough of the smell of cows, so took my lunch box and mug of tea to a barn. Sitting as comfortably as I could on a sack of potatoes, I saw a dark shape run silently along the top of the sacks opposite me. Other rats followed and seemed to play and frisk about, sometimes stopping to eat. I threw a potato in their direction, but missed. I threw a few more, improving my aim, but they were too quick and each missile was neatly dodged. Nothing frightened them off and eventually it was me who moved to finish my lunch in peace, back in the byre.

One job I enjoyed at first, was feeding the bull calf. He had been suckled by his mother for some time and didn't want to feed any other way. I used to put my fingers in his mouth and guide his head down to the bucket of milk whilst he sucked them. It was very satisfying to see how he enjoyed it, he recognized the routine and would bound forward, his big beautiful eyes bright with pleasure, to thrust his head into the bucket. He grew bigger and stronger and was soon onto feed instead of milk. It was no longer a pleasure to feed him as he would get frisky and bound about. He had grown to a considerable size now and bellowed loudly. I would wait until he was at the back of his box before I would dash in, drop the feed into his manger, then bolt for the door and the safety beyond.

Often whilst I worked, I'd notice a great surge of activity when word said 'The Boss' or 'The Missus' were around. Only the chauffeur and the gardener had the confidence to maintain their steady pace in their presence. Even their sons either worked harder or got quickly out of sight. It was said there was a horse-whip hanging in the house to encourage their compliance.

Mark seemed to be the only one doing general farm work, the other sons were in his other businesses and their daughter did the office work.

One day the cowman said I wasn't to feed the bull anymore, the 'Missus' had said so. I was relieved, but it confirmed my suspicion that the Boss and his Missus observed their workers without being seen. I had tried to keep my growing fear of the bull to myself and feed him only when I thought no one was around to witness my turn of speed that I thought would have done credit to a matador.

Chapter seven

Life in the Village.

The hard wintry weather stayed with us, so we girls had to find ways of keeping warm. We laid our working clothes between our blankets to keep the chill off them at night and copied the farmers, who threw a Hessian sack over their shoulders to keep the wind and rain off and tied a boot lace round their dungaree legs to keep the draughts out. The best idea though was to cut a waistcoat from 'thermogene' wadding. This pink cotton wool like material could be bought at the chemist's shop and worn next to the skin to keep warm. As the weather improved we plucked pieces off it until it was so thin we could discard it without missing it.

Our hostel full of girls had made an impact in the village. People were cautious at first, some hostile of our presence and not as kind and friendly as Jack and his wife. As our social life became more organized though, with the occasional dance in the recreation room, the young men from the village and the farmers' sons came along to quickstep and waltz. We would all sing the 'Aye Aye Conga' as we wound our way round in a crocodile. The young men stamped around in a circle for the 'Paul Jones,' then partnered the girl next to them when the music stopped, for the next dance. Then the 'Paul Jones' would play again and we'd have fresh partners for the next one. They were happy friendly evenings and no one grumbled at the ten-o-clock finish as we knew we'd all have to be up early for the next day's work.

The villagers were gradually accepting us, which was quite a compliment considering their cautious ways, as they even looked on people from the next village as foreigners.

One farmer suggested that our hostel would be a good place to hold Young Farmers' Club meetings and many of our girls joined. There were interesting talks and lively debates, sometimes we were invited to visit farms to inspect new machinery and learn how to judge cattle.

Some of the girls had specialized jobs such as rat catching or tractor driving. They'd be hired out among farmers who needed their help and got paid slightly more than general farm workers. "Twenty two and bloody six," I remember one saying as she looked in disgust at her pound note two shilling piece and a sixpence. Not a lot for a hard week's work, but more than others got for the same effort.

Chapter eight

The Litter.

By now I was confident doing most jobs around the farm. I could harness a horse, back it into the shafts and drive a cart. I could milk cows, haul hundred-weight sacks, pluck a chicken and had even come to love the ferocious looking sow and her litter.

I remember when she had lain on her side and pushed fourteen piglets into the world with great heaving and much grunting. It had been my first experience as a midwife and I'd felt very much alone, with a great sense of responsibility as I'd sat with her on the clean straw bedding I'd put down for her. She would lift her huge head and thump it back on the ground, her feet and shoulders twitching and trembling as she struggled to give birth.

How I had hoped that nothing would go wrong as I tried to remember the instructions from the 'Missus'. It was warm and sheltered in the sty and I could hear birds outside scavenging in the troughs, whilst the breeze brought in the scent of nettle shoots and new grass, to mingle with the smell of muddy earth, straw and damp wood.

I'd been getting quite anxious as the sow had been lying there for ages without making any apparent progress, when suddenly the first piglet arrived. What a tiny, perfect, beautiful little creature it was. I snapped the cord and lifted it gently, greased its little tail with Vaseline as I'd been told to prevent it falling off, then put it to suckle at its mother. After the second and third piglets were born it got pretty hectic, as they came as quickly as I could handle them and make sure they could breathe and suckle. I had no time to be anxious now, or to be aware of external sounds or scents, because soon there were fourteen healthy little piglets. Fortunately all went well and a deep contentment settled in that little wooden pigsty at the far end of the three cornered field. The sow lay breathing peacefully, already gathering her strength, her little piglets oozing drops of milk from their mouths. It was a very happy Land Girl who returned to the house to make her report.

Chapter nine

Going to the Blacksmiths.

One day as I was getting on with routine and minding my own business, the Boss called me over to where he was holding a big Clydesdale horse. "Now then, ah think thou wilt manage this yin all right," he said, and gave me instructions to take it to be shod, but not to the village smithy, to the one beyond the opposite hill, some four miles away.

With a few words of encouragement and fewer instructions, I was given a leg up to the saddle. With the horse's head pointing in the right direction down the lonnen, I set off. As usual, I never got a lesson in anything, just some skimpy instructions before getting on with it. He'd said something about "hod on with yer knees," but my legs were stretched wide by the saddle. The ground was a long way below me, I could see over the tops of the hedges, but could barely see spring's early daffodil shoots from that height. Suddenly a chattering blackbird darted out of the hedge in front of us and the big horse sidestepped. It gave me a nasty jolt, but I managed to hang on and my confidence was returning by the time we reached the open road and turned to go down the bank. Now this was something I hadn't bargained for, the horse was angled downhill and I was in danger of sliding off the saddle onto its neck. Remembering the words "hod on to its heed," I tightened the rein slightly to bring its head up. Its hind quarters were moving in an unusually bumpy way, its hooves slipping on the road's shiny surface. No one had thought to warn me that horses walked with a cross-legged gait when going down a steep slippery slope to stop their back feet from skidding.

Having negotiated the hill and the bridge at the bottom, I was beginning to feel more relaxed about going up the other side. I knew it would be easier to bend forward and hang on to a horse going uphill as its head would be up too. This was becoming quite an experience for my first time on horseback! All continued well and I managed to hold it steady as we entered the village, then an upstairs window opened and someone shook a duster. The horse reared, its fore legs clawing the air, it put its head down then kicked out its hind legs as far as they'd go. I can't remember hitting the ground, but there I was. All was quiet, and the horse was still there, thank goodness it hadn't bolted. A slim middle-aged woman was offering me comfort and help. She was obviously not the owner of the offending duster who had disappeared from view, along with any other villagers who'd witnessed my Wild West performance.

My new friend helped me to my feet and though bruised and shaken, I found that fortunately I wasn't hurt. We chatted about the incident and pondered how I would remount the horse. She had an educated voice and invited me to visit her one evening, which I later did with my friend Sarah. We spent some pleasant evenings at her house chatting over cups of tea. We discovered that she was a teacher, who also wrote poetry, she gave us both signed books of her poems of the dale.

I couldn't get back on the horse however, as she was too frail to give me a leg up, neither could we get the nervous horse to stand still. We concluded that it would be best to walk the horse until I came across a man who could help. There were plenty around the local blacksmiths' willing to help, so I was soon back on, but as the horse was unsettled and inclined to shy at passing traffic, I dismounted a mile later and we walked the rest of the way.

The town blacksmith was a strong, capable looking man who eyed the horse with experienced authority. He talked to it softly and stroked it whilst leading it gently but firmly to the square shed where it was securely tethered. I was fascinated by all the equipment neatly stacked around the walls. Most of the tools were large and heavy and his muscles were a tribute to his trade.

19

He ran his hand down the horse's neck and withers, then down a foreleg picking it up to examine the hoof. Talking encouragingly all the time, he progressed to the back feet, lifting each in turn. With his back to the horse, he cupped the hind foot between his knees to remove the old shoe and to file the hard nail like growth around the hoof. He brought a new shoe from the furnace, then hammered and tapped it to a perfect fit ready to fasten with the nails.

Perhaps it was the sizzling sound that upset the great beast; for once again he lashed out with both feet. The startled smith was thrown some distance and as he picked himself up the horse went into its bucking and rearing act. The noise was terrible, it broke its halter and bucked all round the shed, kicking tools and upsetting containers of nails. We watched from safety beyond the door, dodging as missiles came flying out. The horse had gone berserk, a wild creature, with frenzied feet.

It was some time before the din subsided and I didn't need to enter to imagine the havoc it had wrought. The smith told me to go into town for an hour, then calmly and resolutely re-entered his shed to finish the job. How he did it remains a mystery, but when I returned the horse was fully shod and waiting. With a few choice comments about the Boss and his bloody horses, he advised me to "walk the big bugger home," which I'd already decided was my intention!

Strangely, that was the last time I was ever expected to ride one of the Boss's horses, and guessed that the smith had something to do with it.

Chapter ten

Muck Spreading.

The winter wheat was pushing its way up strong and green, as spring brought a surge of activity to the land. Ditches were cleared and cattle driven to more outlying pasture. Now we had to get the land in good heart, which meant spreading muck. This job was allocated to Mark, Eddy and myself, I enjoyed working with them, we were a good team.

Eddy was a ginger haired lad, about twenty years old and quick tempered. Mark was amiable and easy going. They both had a sharp sense of humor and a cheerful attitude, which lightened strenuous or boring work.

A great pile of manure had been accumulated during winter, a rich blend of cow and horse dung, mixed with bedding straw. While one of us held the horse steady, the others loaded the cart. When it was full, we walked the horse to the field where we stood on the load and using five pronged forks, slung the muck around to cover the land section by section.

The return journey was always hilarious, as we tried to keep our balance standing in the empty cart whilst the horse cantered over bumpy ground. It was a rough and dirty journey and we'd argue about whose turn it was to open and close the several gates. Whenever the horse lifted its tail to break wind one of the boys would yell a warning so we'd slither to the sides, out of range.

Loading up wasn't as much fun as spreading the muck. As we lifted the layers off the stack it released a richer pungent smell as we got deeper into it. It didn't affect our appetites though, for despite the lack of water for washing hands we relished our sandwiches with genuine hunger and appreciation.

Chapter eleven

Looking Out.

Spring was also the time to repair dry-stone walls and fences, so I was sent up the hill at the back of the farm to help a wily old countryman do the job. He taught me the rudiments of stone walling, how to lay a firm broad base, how to overlap the stones, how to infill the center and finally to top it off neatly. Some of the stones weighed a great deal and it was a struggle to get them into place. He also taught me how to position fence posts and swing the heavy mallet, letting the handle slip gently in my grip on impact, to avoid feeling the jolt.

It was hard work but we enjoyed the bracing air and the good view. All around we could see men working with tractors or horses and Jack with his two well matched Shire horses plowing the fertile soil in the valley. It was a timeless, ageless scene, where I felt suspended in time with an aerial view of history.

My companion could have stepped from a history book too. He was tall, lean, stiff and gnarled, with an unruffled philosophical view of life. He wore moleskin trousers and heavy rough boots, with an old thick jacket. He never rushed at a job, but approached everything at a steady pace "Do your job well," he said, "but always leave a little bit for tomorrow, no use working yourself out of a job." He taught me to use my eyes, to scan the spaces between the hedges and trees of distant roads for a hint of sun reflecting off glass, for that, he said, could be the Boss's Rolls Royce and he'd be watching us through his binoculars. He taught me to watch the birds too, for if they were disturbed it could be that the Boss was in the vicinity.

Sometimes he would wave his arms over the whole scene and say "Most of this belongs to the Boss and much more that is far away." Then, he would ponder upon the lands and the wealth of that particular man and relate with relish that by rights he should not have been born. His father and mother weren't married, he wasn't only illegitimate, but a penniless illegitimate; and now he owns so much, a very rich and successful man indeed.

Chapter twelve

Pig Driving.

My family of piglets was growing rapidly. They were also joining their mother in the race to reach the swill bucket at feeding time. Although I'd helped her bring her family into the world, the old sow still regarded me with suspicion when they were around, so I treated her with caution and respect. If she wandered around the sty out of sight however, I would pick up a little one for a quick cuddle and when she was fed and docile with a full stomach, I would talk to her and stroke her.

Mucking out their sty was not as unpleasant a task as one would expect, for pigs are clean animals that do not 'dirty' where they sleep or eat. They really appreciate clean bedding too, pushing it into comfortable heaps with their snouts.

One day the Boss said the sow was ready for the boar, so equipped with a long stick, I was sent to drive her there. We went along the road to the village, across the bridge, up the hill and along the road to a distant farm. People stopped and stared, engrossed in the diversion of watching a girl trying to walk a grunting, darting pig through the streets. She tried every mean trick that she could, doubling back and running to each side of the road in the hope of slipping away. She investigated garden gates, her beady little eyes looking greedily at the leaves and flowers beyond her reach. If she spied an open gate it was a race between us, which was imperative that I won. It's surprising how fast a determined pig can run.

A good hour of that erratic journey later, we were at the side road leading to the farm and of course that was the only road so far that she did not intend to investigate. She put on a fine turn of speed and shot onward up the bank. Eventually, hot and breathless, I managed to turn her and we ran into the farmyard. The farmer looked at me with aristocratic disdain and took the pig away. I found a place to sit and wipe my perspiring face, to gather strength for the return journey. How I longed for a drink, but the farmer looked unapproachably arrogant. Though he obviously classed himself as gentry, I was calling both him and the pig by other names.

My Boss and his Missus were in a jocular mood when we returned to the farm. I was given a mug of tea and questioned about the antics of the pig, amongst great guffaws of laughter. "Did it tek then, dost thou think?" queried the Boss. I sincerely hoped so as I did not relish the thought of a return journey.

The next day, I heard a loud bovine noise coming from a loose box, "What's up?" I asked. "Cow come a-bulling" was the reply. Thinking of my recent experience, I hoped I wasn't going to be involved in fetching the bull or walking the cow through the village.

Chapter thirteen

Country Knowledge.

By working in the fields and outlying areas I got to know more of the workforce and had adopted their ways and their dialect. I fitted in by politely assuming either deafness or innocence when ribald jokes were tossed around and gained the men's respect by working hard. Most were decent enough, though there were a couple of them I was happier avoiding.

Though not given to wasting words, other than in fluent cursing when tempers were raised, these men were highly skilled and knowledgeable in many aspects of agriculture and rural life; and could easily move from one job to another.

They could gauge the weather and its effects on crops, they knew about their animals, their behavior, ailments and cures. Their rough hands could bait a hook, or squeeze a warble fly from under an animal's skin and assess the quality of soil by running it through their fingers.

From the most delicate of tasks to the most arduous, these men were capable and competent. It struck me how misguided those 'townies' were who just thought they were 'bumpkins' and didn't understand how skilled they were.

It's a shame we lost some of our ancestors' wisdom during the industrial revolution, when people were lured to the towns with hopes of prosperity. Though education has helped some of them rise above the smoke and squalor, it's their country cousins who have retained the instinct to survive in circumstances where the allegedly more civilized among us, would fail.

Chapter fourteen

Haymaking.

As the days lengthened, our valley became lush and green. Clouds of midges cavorted by the river whilst bees buzzed from flower to flower. The air filled with insect life, their droning mingled with bird song and the impatient cheeping of the fledglings waiting to be fed. Ascending skylarks trilled whilst thrushes sought out snails to smash their shells on stones.

Even the ground was crawling with life. I was fascinated by the ants as they scurried back and forth, carrying or tugging something to their nest. There were iridescent beetles shining in the sunlight, caterpillars munching their way along the leaves and dancing butterflies dipping over the fragrant and beautiful flowers of the hay meadow.

I was sent to the farm further up the hill, to clear up stones and repair boundaries. This was one of the Boss's farms, where Ted and his wife Freda, lived. They were a really nice couple, happy, light hearted and generous with pudding and tea to go with my sandwiches, which I enjoyed around the friendly atmosphere of their table.

They were about two miles from the village and sometimes when I was working in the fields I would see Freda stoically climbing the steep road there, laden with shopping.

She invited me to visit after work and sometimes I'd go there after the evening meal, to sit by the fire with them on the high backed wooden bench that was part of the inglenook. They were happy evenings and I always enjoyed the walk home in the dusk, when I would see the twinkling lights of the village as I walked down the hill. I thought life was pleasant then, but I suspected that harder times would lie ahead.

As the season progressed, there was much discussion about the state of the hay and the weather, judging the critical time for harvesting. Eventually the big decision was made, so Jack was sent to open up the field with his scythe, ready for the tractor and the mower coming in. Where the wind had battered the hay to the ground, Jack would slip his scythe's blade under, to cut it. When his blade went blunt, I took it to the corner of the field where the tools lay and sharpened it.

As the cut hay lay neatly on its side, we walked along the rows turning them with hay rakes to let the warm air through. We did this every day until it was dry enough to be heaped into haycocks. As these dried they were heaped together to form a stack about the height of a man. This was taken away on a horse drawn bogey to the big stack, where hay was forked to a man working on the top. He'd place it quickly and carefully, paying special attention to the corners and sides, so his stack would be strong and straight.

During the haymaking season, our working day extended with the hours of daylight. All of the farm's routine work had to be attended to as usual though, so as we worked we watched the sky, as an unexpected shower could undo a lot of progress and mean more days of backbreaking raking, turning, and forking, for us.

Tea breaks were a special feature of hay and harvest time, when baskets of sandwiches and scones were carried to the field to sustain the workers. I was often called upon to carry the heavy baskets, or to help cut and butter the loaves of bread. It took several loaves, as there could be up to a dozen or so workers, hot, tired and needing refreshment. When we had the opportunity to do so, we would sit by the hedge, appreciating the shade and any cool breeze, whilst easing our aching backs.

Tea breaks did not last long, the weather was a hard taskmaster and so was the Boss. There were long evenings of work after tea, before sunset released us from our labors and we could head off to home and bed.

During the long sweaty days of summer, bitten by flies and midges,

I would sometimes think of the cold winter days with their biting winds howling down the dale. I'd wonder which was worse, for the heat of an unyielding sun in a field with no shade, could be very exhausting.

Eventually, the last fork full of hay was tossed to the top of the stack and the gate closed on the last field. I looked back over the shaven fields with the sun sinking over the horizon and felt a great satisfaction, with relief that the hay was in. I hoped I would have my evenings back for resting, reading, and writing letters, until the grain harvest in the autumn.

Chapter fifteen

The Roundup.

The Boss had over a hundred Galloway ponies running wild in an allotment on the high moors to the north of the village. Occasionally they were rounded up and selected for breaking in, or to work in the pits.

One morning, I was sent with Mark, Eddy, Old Bill and a boy, three miles to the top of the moors, to round up the ponies and bring them down to the farm for selection. The three men were on horseback, whilst I had to walk with the boy. We were happy and relaxed, looking forward to the excitement as we journeyed up the hill. I found that the 'allotment' was the size of a large farm, with a farmhouse, a stream and a stonewall boundary. The ponies were scattered over the upper reaches and our aim was to round them up and shepherd them through the gate to the road, for the long walk back to the farm.

Those on horseback set off at a gallop with Old Bill's collie dog darting around them. Their purpose was to get ahead of the horses and turn them down the field towards the road. Hearing the thudding of hooves and the excited cowboy yells of the two younger men, the ponies tossed their manes and galloped madly around. Luckily the perimeter walls kept them from galloping too far away, but the chase was on. It felt just like a rodeo as they galloped wildly about the fell, some breaking away from the main group, which me the dog and the boy, had to chase back. Once, all the Galloways were stretched in a single file, a hundred of them galloping hard, silhouetted along the skyline with the mounted men galloping alongside them. It was an impressive sight.

Eventually they headed down towards us. We hoped to stand our ground with our sticks, somewhat nervously clenched, as the column came nearer at great speed. There was one man at the back of them and one at each side, whilst the dog darted around chasing any back that attempted to break away. When the ponies saw the open gate with me and the boy at either side of it, they turned to make a final dash for freedom. 'Get after the buggers' the men yelled, 'turn them, run!' We did run, waving our sticks, our feet getting caught in clumps of heather, we ran shouting and yelling, while the men tried to steady the main part of the column, which was getting increasingly excited and restless. Sweating and swearing we ran, our task seemingly impossible, when a shout of "jump the bloody wall," told me that some had got through the gateway and onto the road. I scrambled quickly over, just in time to stop them galloping off along the highway.

Walking at the head of a column of sturdy, kicking ponies is no mean feat. They were right there behind me, pushing forwards all the time, always trying to trot past in a bid for freedom. I had to dart from one side of the road to the other, brandishing my stick and hoping to intimidate those fearless little animals. As the grass verge widened, I was relieved to see a horseman come to the front, then by the time we reached the crossroads, the boy had joined me so we were able to take our stand at the road ends, to turn the ponies in the right direction. Now it was downhill towards the village we could see in the valley below, all we needed to do was look out for open gates and side roads.

I turned to take in the scene behind us. What a magnificent sight it was with the jostling, kicking ponies tossing their beautiful long manes and long silken tails, the men on horseback; and what a clatter of hooves!

People stopped to look as we went through the village and traffic halted as our cavalcade passed by. When they were all herded into the farmyard, the Boss came to view them. Mark, Eddy and the boy, had great fun trying to get on their backs but the ponies bucked and reared, whilst the boss shouted encouragement. One of the smallest of them had them off its back before they got properly seated; it was its speed that did the trick. The fun of the rodeo lasted some time, with much laughter and many bruises, before they were herded into a field for the night. Next day the buyers came to the farm, so our final task was to take those they'd bought to the station and herd them into trucks. The lucky ones that hadn't been sold went back to the moor, whilst the others would probably be sent down a pit to haul coal. The beauty and freedom of the high moors would be just a distant memory for them during their long stint in the dark pit.

Chapter sixteen

Harvest.

High summer was bowing to autumn gold; ripening fields of corn bordered by berried hedges, topped by purple heathery moors, gave a new visual aspect to our valley.

I had always loved the country and wanted to live there and now this was my valley, for I loved it dearly. Had the Prince Bishops who rode and hunted in this beautiful valley loved it as I did? To them it would have been a playground, an arena for their sport, whilst the land would have provided them with income to add to their wealth. I loved it for its beauty, its seasons, trees, flowers, birds and insects. I loved its people and way of life, down to the soil under my feet.

Now the corn stood high, lifting its golden ears to a golden sun. Jack prepared the scythes for sharpening, ready to open the fields, whilst Eddy got the reaper ready for hitching onto the tractor. Soon the gate to the field was opened and harvesting commenced. Where the corn had been flattened it was cut with a scythe and tied into sheaves by hand. Once that job was done, we joined the others who were stacking sheaves into stooks, to dry. The tractor went round and round the field, followed by a band of stookers. The central island of uncut corn was shrinking all the time. As it got smaller, the more densely it was packed with rabbits that, frightened by the tractor and the long run over the stubble, crowded into the center. Eventually the tractor left them no option but to run for safety, then the chase began. Men with pitchforks and stones gleefully chased the poor things, and the field became a scene of great activity.

Eddy jumped off his tractor and joined in, the yelling and cheering spurred the rabbits on and very few were caught. Those who caught them were pleased for the opportunity to supplement their rations.

We spent many days like this, following the reaper and setting up the stooks with their East and West ends open so the prevailing wind would blow through to dry them. When the Boss was satisfied with their condition they were taken to the thresher. This was run by Black Bart, who traveled the Dales with his machine. He was massively muscular, with black hair and a beard streaked with black dribbles of tobacco. He seemed aptly named, the more so for having a surly expression as black as thunder too.

There was an elevator by the side of the thresher, which took the sheaves to the top where a man fed them in. It was a continuous motion from forking the sheaves on at the bottom, to grain coming out the top to drop into sacks, which were tied and loaded onto a cart to be taken to a barn for storage. We were constantly raking away the chaff and the muck and we were soon as dirty as any coal miners. "You'll be spitting blackcocks tonight lass," they joked.

Relentlessly the machine churned on and relentlessly we forked, pitched, lifted, tied, loaded and raked, with sweat and muck covered faces. There was a shout of "hi-up there," as the great drive belt flew off the engine and whizzed through the air. "Just about took me bloody head off" yelled one, "could have killed someone" said another, "thout there were a nasty smell." Black Bart never said a word.

Soon all was back to normal, the machine working smoothly again with Black Bart shoveling coal into its boiler and spitting baccy.

I looked at the scene before me, pale golden fields, the flowing river and birds flying overhead. The engine and its thresher were the center of activity, with tractors and horses bringing in sheaves for threshing whilst others took the filled sacks away.

I thought how different this scene of rural English fields would be from that on the continent, where our boys were fighting on fields that were battle torn, for the continuation of our freedom and our future harvests.

Walking along the lonnen from the farm, I would peep through gaps in the hawthorn hedge to look down on the Station Master's garden. I could see he had a very good crop of apples, but one day they'd gone. Mark, the Boss's son was cheerfully boasting that he'd scrumped them, but his joviality didn't last long, as I heard that the Boss had reached for his horsewhip when he heard.

Their own garden had a good crop of apples, as well as flowers, fresh vegetables and other fruits for the family. The gardener was a pleasant man who went quietly about his work, listening to the birds and observing nature. He taught me to recognize the song of the Yellow Bunting as 'a little bit of bread and no cheese'. His wife had a long term illness; and one day he asked me if I'd like to come to tea, to meet her. They were a quiet, contented couple, but I felt very sorry for them as I returned to the hostel, as his wife was so tired and frail.

The Chauffeur was a more confident and ebullient character, who must have had a very interesting time driving his boss around the various businesses and coping with his ever changing moods. He was polishing the Rolls one day, when the Missus called me. She was irritable following a phone call to the butcher. "Go quickly in the Rolls to the village, to pick up a parcel of meat from the butcher," I was told. I looked at my dirty hands, the chauffeur noticed and winked. I climbed into the front seat, where out of sight of the Missus we both laughed at the contrast of a smart uniformed chauffeur in a gleaming black Rolls Royce and me in dungarees and heavy boots, dirty and tousled, so handsomely escorted.

The butcher was all smiles and apologies as I entered his shop and he left off serving his other customers to hand me the parcel. I wish I could have heard what the Missus had said to command such immediate attention!

Our Boss had put some big Shire horses in a field at the back of the farm, so they could have a rest from their heavy forestry work. As things were dying down for the winter there wasn't much nourishment for them in the short grass, so I had to take buckets of oats to put in troughs in the field where they grazed. The field was on a slope and it was a steep uphill struggle to their troughs. The first time I did it, I got to the troughs and emptied the buckets shouting "caa-hop, caa-hop, caa-hop," and had time to get well out of the way before they galloped down. Not so the next time however, or ever again after that! They kept a look out for me, and as I plodded up the hill with the buckets, they would come galloping down. Before I could reach the trough they were bearing down on me, skidding on the wet grass, unable to stop for several yards. Their height of eighteen hands appeared double because of the steepness of the slope and I was convinced I would be crushed by their great bodies or tangled in their legs, as they slid past missing me by inches.

It was time to pick potatoes, Jack and the horses went ahead to bring them to the surface, while Mark, Eddy and I, with sacks tied round our waists to form large pockets to put them in, followed. We started at the bottom of the rows and worked our way up, filling large sacks left at row ends as we progressed. Bent double, we scrabbled in the muddy soil to harvest them and after a few hours it was painful to straighten our backs. Bent again, we plodded on, "heads down and arses up," laughed Eddy. Though we were muddy and uncomfortable and there was a chilling wind blowing, our morale was high as we chatted and joked. It was a poor harvest though; the potatoes weren't in good condition. The Boss came along to look at them, "Good enough for town folks," he said. Seething with anger, I wondered if I dare say something. Too late, he'd already walked away, jauntily swinging his horsewhip.

The Boss had acquired a baler, so when Black Bart returned with his thresher, the baler was positioned to catch the straw which was thumped along a square horizontal tunnel, until it emerged solid and compacted, ready to expand to tighten its wires and weighing eight stone.

My job was to stand at the side of the tunnel and push the heavy dividing bars in at intervals, to thread strong wire through them. Then I had to run round to the other side, return the wire, run back to knot it and push another bar in. If I was lucky, I'd have a boy to help return the wires to me. The work had to be done quickly and accurately, the noisy thumping sounded a steady rhythm to set the pace.

We were glad of our breaks, mid morning and lunchtime, when we could ease our parched and dusty throats from our flasks and tea bottles.

Some of the workers were curious about my home life and my boyfriend Bob, who was in the D.E.M.S. (Defense Equipment Merchant Ships) as an army gunner seconded to the merchant navy. When he had leave, the Boss gave me time off. This had surprised and offended many of his workers who said they couldn't get a day off for their mother's funeral! I was a loner among the men, always a little wary, having to distance myself, yet willing to be affable and glad of their friendship. Most important of all, I had to gain their respect both as a woman and as a worker, as the highest accolade one could gain in the dale, was to be acknowledged as a good worker.

Our break was soon over, and we were back on the job with the baler thumping out its dust and seeds into our faces. It was hard work and tempers frayed, with much swearing at each other and the machine.

At night I lay coughing in my bunk, my hands and wrists aching from tying endless knots. I hoped the baling would soon be completed, but then the Boss contracted us out to other farms and it wasn't until the season was completely over that I felt clean again.

Chapter seventeen

Time Off.

With the harvest safely in, we Land Girls could all look forward to weekends at home. After work on a Saturday morning we would put on our best uniforms of breeches, overcoat and hat, pack a case, then queue at the village bus stop. The bus traveled from the top of the dale, to the small town at the far end, from where we could get buses to our home areas.

Our ride in the dales bus was a jolly experience, everyone knew each other and the driver would joke with his passengers. There was laughter and a really happy atmosphere. Gossip was exchanged and many a date made, as hopeful lads asked "ist thar coming to the dance?"

The bus was small and always full, people 'strap hanging' swaying as it negotiated the winding country roads.

Sometimes I took a friend home with me; and mother would bake a batch of deliciously light and yeasty tea cakes. We always enjoyed them, but we were lucky if we got a piece with a currant in, as they were luxuries. In return, I visited friends' homes and they were always happy and interesting weekends, which deepened my appreciation of family ties and loyalties. I wondered how some of their parents managed to eke out their meager rations to feed us with uncomplaining hospitality, as they didn't have gardens to grow any vegetables. When I visited Jane's neat little terrace house where we shared a big bed in a tiny bedroom, her loving mother came and tucked us in and kissed us goodnight, as if we were both her long lost infants.

If I ever had to stay at the hostel for a weekend, Jack's wife would invite me for Sunday dinner, which was the big meal of the week. It started with Yorkshire pudding and gravy. About seven large loaf tins would come out of the oven, with the puddings risen high over their tops. One was tipped onto each plate, though the younger children would have one between them. Jack would eat any surplus. Then the meat was carved and served up with more gravy and fresh vegetables from Jack's allotment. The table was covered with a clean tablecloth on Sundays and it was delightful to see all the children's bonny little faces around it.

The cloth was removed after the meal to be replaced by a large enamel bowl for washing up the great pile of dishes, tins and sooty pans. Everyone helped except Jack, who could enjoy the luxury of an afternoon's sleep.

When the chores were finished, we would stroll along the road and through some fields. Jack's wife knew the names of every flower and the children gathered posies to take home. We sauntered back in time to feed the family pig down on Jack's allotment. It was a Large White, well cared for and friendly, we all stroked it and talked to it, but the children said that Daddy had told them not to get fond of it, as it would be killed before winter.

Chapter eighteen

Plowing.

A spell of good weather seemed a good opportunity to thoroughly clean the byre and horseboxes. So, I was given a bucket, a brush, a large amount of Snowcem; and told to get a ladder and whitewash the byre walls. As I'd been brought up in a bungalow, I wasn't used to climbing tall ladders and the gable ends were very high! I clung tightly to the ladder as I slapped the Snowcem on. Not having done anything like this before, I was pleasantly surprised at the result, but not so pleased that the Missus also praised my work and said I would always be given that job in the future. When she suggested that I might like a bite of dinner, my spirit lifted though, as my stomach yearned for the food that was sending out that tantalizing smell. "Tip your bait into the pig swill," she said, which I gladly did, thinking it was the best place for it.

Never before had I been in such company. There assembled were the rosy cheeked Missus who was dishing out platefuls of steaming hot food, her sister who helped in the house, the sons, Mark and Tom who ran his father's sand and gravel business, Flora, the Boss's daughter who worked in the office at the sawmill, all seated round the table with The Boss himself. The Boss enquired about various aspects of his business, his Missus made some dry comments and I was asked about my home life, office work and what my father did. They'd already asked me about Bob; when I'd wanted time off when he was on leave.

As I had to help with the dishes and tidy up after the meal, there was no chance to rest for the remainder of my dinner hour, but I didn't mind, with a good meal inside of me.

All the remains were consigned to the pig swill. I thought of all the hungry people elsewhere who had to queue for anything that would make a meal and how the food would always run out after the first half of the queue was served, so the women would have to run to another queue and hope for better luck.

The good food in the pigswill was still in my mind when I collected the eggs that afternoon. I slipped one into my pocket, intending to take one a day for my mother and Bob's. A cow kicked me at milking time though and squashed the egg, which ran slowly down my trouser leg. Hastily I swilled it away, glad that no one had seen, but I got some funny looks later and I guessed they thought I'd wet myself. I'd been brought up to be honest, so it looked like honest I would remain.

Before I had time to get used to the good dinners at the farm, the Boss told me to go to an allotment about three miles to the south of the dale. This was up the hill past the farm where Ted and Freda lived and on and on uphill until the land flattened out on top, then a little way further over the other side. We were beyond 'farmland' and into areas of bracken, heather and coarse grass. There was plenty of sky up there, with wide panoramic views and stands of conifers.

A rough track left the road and led me to the two hundred acre allotment, it was a most beautiful place, the coarse heather land sloped down to a stony stream, backed by dark pinewood. All the country around was natural and splendid, whilst in the distance was a well cared for lodge, nestled among conifers and with rhododendrons at its frontage.

The Boss was standing beside a brand new yellow caterpillar tractor, chatting to Mark and Eddy. "Now then," the Boss said to me, "thous gonna plow." The controls of the tractor were simple enough to learn and the boys had put markers up so I could drive in a straight line. A three furrowed plow was hitched up, which Eddy had to stand on whilst it was moving, to stop it bouncing up whenever it hit a stone. "Tek her away, let her go," commanded the Boss, so off I went, the tractor jerking as its tracks encountered larger stones. I could hear Eddy cursing his bumpy ride, but I kept my eye on the markers as I drove towards the pinewood. At the end, I lifted the plow and turned the tractor to look down the furrow. The clumps of heather and lumps of stone made it look untidy, but not bad I thought. So feeling reasonably pleased, I headed for the small group at the end of the furrow. They were muttering and laughing, "It's like dog piss int snaw," shouted the Boss waving his horse whip at my furrow.

That was the first day of many weeks spent on the allotment, I got used to the long walks in the early morning and at night. Parts of the road were so steep that my boots slipped and rolled on the gravel, but at each bend there were magnificent views, whilst in the spring, the rhododendrons came into abundant flower around the lodge. No one was ever seen there, but it was rumored that the owner had a pet fox.

My plowing improved and I became adept at handling the tractor. Mark, Eddy and I took turns at the uncomfortable job of standing on the plow and one day when the tractor stopped suddenly as the plow hit a stone, I was flung off and hit my nose on some metal. The boys were concerned as it bled freely, so I bathed it in the cold clear waters of a spring, whilst Mark and Eddy prized the stone out of the ground with iron bars.

There was a cabin by the river on the allotment, where we could eat our sandwiches. If Mark was there he would sometimes give me one of his tasty ones, with ham or a whole fried egg, as a swap for one of mine. 'Castleside ham' he called mine, meaning jam; and unless he was very hungry he usually gave me it back, which I gladly ate to appease my hunger.

While we were on the allotment that spring and early summer, there were lots of thunder storms. We usually sheltered in the cabin, but once there was a violent storm when I was on my own and a long way from shelter, so I lay under the tractor to keep dry. The nearby pinewood stood black against a glowering sky till the lightning illuminated the whole scene. At times like this, with the threatening energy of nature circling the hills, one felt very much alone.

If we got a soaking, we just had to dry out in the wind, hopefully with the help of some sun. When the storms passed, I would wipe the tractor's seat as best I could and carry on with the job. There were no driver's cabs, or safety bars in those days.

After plowing, the discs were used to cut the sods of earth into smaller pieces, which were left to weather until early summer when they were harrowed.

A day came when the sun beat down mercilessly, nothing stirred in the stifling heat and the long hours stretched relentlessly through the day. I was working alone, a hot sweaty blob on a hot diesel tractor, dragging a dusty harrow. The cold spring was my only comfort, where I cooled my hands and burning face with its chilled water and drank it down my parched throat. Relief didn't last long however, and I was frequently having to stop the tractor to refresh myself. Then, a sick dizziness struck me and I vomited. With great concentration I willed my feet to take me to the cabin. It was stifling hot in there but I lay on the floor waiting for the dizziness to pass. No more work got done that day, and in a very weak state I somehow managed the long walk back to the hostel.

A few days later, Mark came out in boils, and his mother dosed him with castor oil. He spent most of that day sprinting for the dry-stone wall and hastily clambering over it to disappear into the pinewood. He always came back red with anger, shaking his fist at Eddy and me, who were convulsed with laughter; and shouted loud encouragement and cheered every time he made it to the wall in time.

I had another spell of working around the Home Farm and by now I was almost accepted as one of the family. I'd often be called upon to help out in the house if things got busy; and found that 'The Missus' was definitely 'The Boss' within the walls of her home. She kept the family in good order and often gave them a good telling off. Her sons were almost twice her height but that did not deter her. She made sure that they removed their Wellington boots before entering, or scraped and wiped their shoes. She was highly indignant once, when Mark thoughtlessly left a spanner on the mantelpiece. After a good dressing down, he sheepishly removed it and went out.

We were having a mug of tea one day when she returned from a Women's institute meeting. The Boss asked "Now lass, how didst tha come on?" She was bristling with anger at a dispute within the committee. "I stood up" she said, and quoted;

> "Oh that the mischief making few,
> Could be reduced to one or two,
> And they be painted red and blue,
> That everyone might know them."

Our Boss roared with laughter, "Thou'd tell em, thou'd show em," he chuckled. His eyes were now focused on us the workers, drinking our hard earned mugs of tea. Silently we moved out, thinking it better to leave her and her ill humor to the Boss.

Chapter nineteen

Bulldozing.

At this stage of the war, farmers were advised to enlarge the size of their fields by knocking out hedges, to increase the yield from their land. This became my job, so my caterpillar tractor had a bulldozer blade fitted to it. Trees were uprooted by either pushing them out with the blade, or by fastening a chain round them and pulling. Occasionally men with crosscut saws had to come to fell them, leaving stumps on which I would use the blade, to push, lift, prize, or whatever was necessary to rid the ground of stumps and roots. When all the rubbish was cleared away, I'd use the blade to spread the soil flat and even. The last move was to drag the blade backwards, just tickling the ground, erasing all track marks and leaving it as smooth as icing on a cake. It was enjoyable, satisfying work, but defacing the countryside, ruining the hedges and the habitat of birds and animals, saddened me.

Sometimes the tractor and blade were sent out on contract work and one day when I reported to Home Farm, The Boss was on the telephone. "All right, aye, I'll send a man along," he was saying. He was in a good mood, chuckling with suppressed laughter. "Gan alang to yin farm and report fer duty," he said. I drove the bulldozer along to the farm, where the farmer looked at me incredulously. "He said he would send a man," he declared, not trying to hide his annoyance. "I am he," I retorted, thinking "I will show him," and I did. I completed a very satisfactory job but got no thanks. In fact I never saw him after our first encounter.

Nobody brought me a mug of tea or asked if I needed anything. Nobody said goodbye as I slammed the tractor into top gear and headed back to home farm when the job was done.

There was a farm just up the hill from ours, where they wanted some fields disking. The farmer was one of our Missus's brothers, but he was either very poor or very mean, I never knew which. His wife was a thin anxious woman, and they had several children. Neither his wife or family ever had a full sized hens egg to eat, only Bantam hen's eggs were used in the house, all the other hens eggs, along with anything else marketable, were sold.

My job would last two days, and at the end of the first I was told to back my tractor and discs into a barn for the night. It was full of sacks of corn and there was just room to accommodate it. The farmer was hopping about anxiously, "left hand down, you might just do it, no, no, right hand down, mind them sacks." From the height of my seat I could see just how I would do it, with five inches to spare either side of the blades. Backing a tractor and trailer had never been a problem for me, so I gave her some throttle, slammed her in, stopped the engine and climbed out. The farmer was jumping around, waving his arms and red in the face. "You could have split them sacks and lost me corn," he expostulated. "But I didn't and an inch is as good as a mile," I tartly replied, secretly enjoying the comedy of the situation. We had an audience of wide-eyed children and a smirking teenage son, all of whom I knew, would enjoy recounting this event.

My tractor and its blade were loaded onto a lorry and taken to the large allotment north of the dale, where the pit ponies grazed. It was a large expanse of moorland, all humps and hollows, sloping down to a stream, then uphill to a dry-stone wall. Good country, with plenty of cover for grouse, curlew and lapwing.

I climbed into the tractor and sat quietly for a few minutes, appreciating the beauty of the surroundings and assessing the situation. My job was to level off the humps and hollows, prize out stones and leave the land cleared and level for plowing.

Having decided where to start, I slipped the tractor into gear and experienced the joy of climbing the humps. The front halves of the tracks reaching upwards, the back half slowly climbing until it was suspended, throttle shut off, see-sawing till the front tracks dropped to the ground while the back tracks went up in the air. Given maximum throttle we roared off to the next hump to be negotiated, skirting any rocks en route and repeating the process until we reached the chosen spot to start work.

When it was lunch time, I carried my bait tin and its frugal contents along to the farmhouse where an employee and his sister were tenants. I was invited in to sit at the table and given a mug of tea. I was agreeably surprised to also be given a bowl of milk pudding. They were not happy living on the moor, preferring softer, flatter country with more trees. They also set me riddles that I could not solve and patronizingly gave me the answers, smiling with their lips but not with their eyes.

What a relief it was to get back to the tractor and let it roar into life.

At the end of each working day I walked half a mile to the road, then the three miles down the hill to the hostel. It was the same road I trudged up early mornings to start the day's work. Occasionally Mark or Eddy came to work on the allotment, but most of the time I was alone.

At ten o'clock time I would sit on the heather and nibble a sandwich, watching the birds and listening to the stream in the dip of the moor. Sheep grazed there, so I'd also watch their steady movements as I sat.

One day Mark and Eddy came and we fired the heather. We restricted the areas to those where it grew tall and dense and sprinkled kerosene to start the blaze. The flames crackled whilst the noxious smoke drifted in the wind.

My tractor was no longer new and increasingly I spent time with the manual in one hand and a spanner in the other, trying to find the problem and get it going again. It was on one of these days that Mark appeared. Having diagnosed the problem as a blockage in the diesel tank, he looked at my hand and grinned, "I've seen babies born with bigger hands than that," he said, "now just pull your sleeve up and put your hand in the tank to fish round for foreign bodies." We must have had a poor consignment of fuel because it happened so frequently that I got a diesel rash right up my arm.

It was a heavy tractor to hand crank, so the only way I could start it was to bring the handle right up, stand on it and jerk it with my foot, this had to be done several times.

Someone told me once that I'd break my bloody leg, but with no offers of help and usually on my own, there was no other way to bring the engine to life. When the weather got colder, Mark showed me how to light a fire under it to warm the diesel.

If I was lucky, one of the Boss's timber wagons would be returning to the saw-mill at night, so I would get a lift part of the way home. There was so little traffic on the road that it was a surprise to see any, and lifts were few and far between. An alternative route that I sometimes took was over the wall and straight across the moor, feeling glad that I was wearing strong boots as a precaution against adders. It was a wild lonely route, startled grouse would flap out of the heather with their warning cry of "go back, go back," and skylarks would rise with soaring song. My favorite was the haunting rippling call of the circling curlew, so with these and the omnipresent sheep, there was plenty to see and hear on the moor.

Eventually I would come to a path that led to a smallholding and continued past its cottage. This led to a better track and onto a road, from where in about a mile, was the hostel, a meal and a bath.

Chapter twenty

Shows and Dancing.

Our social life in the village was quite good, there was the Young Farmers Club and dances and social evenings at the hostel. Dances were also occasionally held in the village hall, where some of the young men of the dale had formed a band. Girls like me, with fiancées in the forces were never left to be wallflowers; we were always asked to dance and would be escorted home by boys who didn't have current girlfriends.

One memorable night a truckload of American soldiers who were posted nearby, came to a dance at our hostel. They were big men, loud talking and exuding confidence; they whisked the girls off their feet and took over the dance floor. They shouted, laughed and twirled the girls about and wouldn't take 'no' for an answer. We couldn't hear the music from the gramophone for the din they created.

Farmers' sons and village lads stood around, initial amusement turning to discontent and frustration. One or two of the girls loved the excitement and were later dating them, but most of us found them loud and brash. Eventually the boys of the dale asked them to leave, they did not protest and were soon hustled outside, but the night was spoilt. The boys took their leave and went home; the girls quietly tidied the room. The Americans never returned.

In the autumn there was a parade, the farmers decorated their horses and carts to parade through the village. It was a great occasion that took a lot of preparation, including a lot of polishing. Mark brought me their best harnesses and brasses and I spent two days sitting on a pile of straw in a loose box, cleaning them to perfection.

Jack chose the quietest Shire horses and washed their fetlocks until the hair was like a shining skirt around their hooves. The horses were brushed and groomed until their coats were gleaming, their beautiful manes were washed and their hooves polished. On the morning of the parade they had their manes and tails plaited with ribbons and the shining harnesses, horse brasses and other colorful decorations were fitted. The carts were being decorated at the same time, with sheaves of corn, ribbons and flowers. They'd been scrubbed clean and painted especially for the occasion. I had great fun decorating our own cart with two of my friends from the hostel, making it bright and cheerful. Finally, with the horse harnessed, we stood on the cart along with Mark and Eddy, 'armed' with our pitchforks as we drove off to join the other entrants for the parade. The entire village turned out to see the procession, the horses were spectacular and the farmers and laborers were justly proud of their efforts.

Our dale also had an annual Agricultural Show with plenty of livestock and judging of cows, bulls, pigs, sheep and horses. There was a sheepdog trial that Old Bill always entered, a popular pets' corner and a Women's Institute Stall. Refreshment was available and the local brass band added its volume to the general entertainment.

There was Cumberland wrestling, where one of the Boss's sons; a great strong hunk of a man entered the competition. They clasped each other round their backs, bodies bent forward and bottoms outwards, each swaying in a display of strength trying to get their opponent to the ground. It was a social occasion for the whole dale and greatly enjoyed by the outlying farmers and their wives. Our Boss was particularly interested in the new machinery on display, he would have a word with people as he walked around, but was usually on his own. His active mind and powerful presence destined him to be a loner.

Chapter twenty-one

Home Visit.

A letter arrived from Bob; he'd been away for two years and was coming home for ten days leave. It seemed unbelievable, that long wait was now at an end. Without stopping to think I rushed round to the farm, luckily the Boss was there and I blurted out my request for leave. "Bugger off yem then," he said, "thars nay bloody good to me when he's yem."

I dashed back to the hostel and started packing. Bob and I lived quite close to each other, so on my weekends home I always visited his mother and often had tea with her on a Saturday afternoon. She was a hospitable lady and her daughters and their families often came too.

The prospect of ten days together had seemed wonderful, but soon those days were slipping swiftly by. We had enjoyed our favorite walks along familiar paths of country and coast again. We had sat looking out over the sea, unable to get near it because the beaches were mined. Some of our field walks were out of bounds too, taken over by the military, with gun emplacements.

Some buildings in the town had been demolished by bombs, leaving gaps in the streets. We visited relatives who were so pleased to see us that they offered whatever hospitality they could give. The war was never discussed; it was the one subject no one wanted to talk about. For a short while, we could forget the past, ignore the future, and enjoy the luxury of comparative peace and idleness.

Unfortunately time did pass, so all too soon we were in the cold, depressing atmosphere of Newcastle station and the last goodbye. There was no knowing when, if ever, we would see each other again. Other khaki clad figures were also boarding the train, their young women waving a fond farewell and mothers holding babies and little children for a goodbye kiss. I hoped they all had happy memories to last them, God willing, to their next leave.

Chapter twenty-two

Back on the Allotment.

Back at the farm, the Boss was not in a good mood, "Thous back," was all he said, and I was sent to the allotment where the bulldozer awaited.

The walk seemed longer, the uphill road, steeper. The allotment, I noted, was not as wild and bonny as when I first saw it. Now it had great patches of leveled off earth and I hoped the wildlife had not suffered too much, especially the ground nesting birds. There were still considerable acres of heather moorland beyond the allotment for them. The wartime policies of the Agricultural Board were responsible for the devastation of a lot of natural beauty; and it was rumored that the Boss would get ten pounds for each acre of land he reclaimed.

With the tractor started and work under way, my mood lifted with the serenity of the scene, the distant horizon of moor meeting sky, the stone walls built by men who belonged to the last century. I wondered if they had loved the uplands the way I loved them. Had they looked around and said to themselves "I lift up mine eyes unto the hills, from whence cometh my strength," as I did in times of distress?

Cumulous clouds drifted over the sky, as the playful breeze patted my face and filled my lungs with pure, sweet air. Optimism reasserted itself; there was no better place to see the war out. As the Government had decreed that two million acres had to be plowed out for food, I thought I had better get on and contribute my two hundred of them.

I left my bait tin by the dry-stone wall and went to examine the new four furrow plow that had been brought to the allotment. As before, someone had to put their weight on it to keep the blades in the ground, so Eddy was sent to help and we took turns. He was a happy person who liked to sing folk songs, his laments rendered in the open air were pleasant to listen to as he had a good voice, but he could be quick tempered and we often argued.

One day when I was driving the tractor and he was on the plow, I saw that a swarm of bees was about to cross our path, en route for the heather. I stopped the tractor intending to wait for the swarm to pass and turned round to explain to Eddy. He was gesticulating wildly, obviously in one of his tantrums. "What the bloody hell have you stopped for?" he yelled. "Bees," I shouted. "Get on," he commanded, "bees wint hurt you, bloody frightened coward." Angered by his unjustified fury I slammed the tractor into top gear and with full throttle I charged through the swarm, keeping my eyes tightly shut. I opened them to see Eddy running speedily past me holding his neck and yelling "buggers got me." His face was distorted with pain and fury as he shook his fist at me. I could not suppress my laughter, nor did I wish to!

Eddy ran to plunge his head into the cold stream, cooling his stings and his temper.

I re-set the plow and congratulated myself that for once, I had not emerged too badly from an argument.

At lunchtime I picked up my bait tin from beside the wall and carried it across to the farm kitchen, where the usual mug of tea was given to me. When I opened the tin though, I found that ants had got into my sandwiches. I tried to pick them out, the brother and sister smiled but showed no sympathy as they tucked into their ample plates of savory smelling dinner. I was famished to despair, so desperately hungry that I contemplated eating a sandwich, ants included, but solemnly drank my cup of tea instead, then said "thank you," for my bowl of milk pudding. I knew I was lucky to get that, but how I longed for a thick crust of bread. The prospect of a long, hard, hungry afternoon, followed by a three-mile walk back to the hostel, was a chilling thought.

When I was chatting to the girls at the hostel that night, I told them about my experience. One of them, a County tractor driver, said that where she was working, she had to sit outside in the cold to eat her sandwiches, but the Italian prisoner of war had been invited indoors and given a good plate of hot dinner.

There were now two gradual slopes running down to the stream, where previously there had been humps and hollows, boggy areas and stony places at the allotment.

The bogs had been a problem to the tractor, as it slipped and slithered on the waterlogged mire. Once when it was sliding sideways at a dangerous angle, Mark shouted "jump, she's gonna coup!" But I managed to maneuver it further down the bog, where it stuck fast. Mark spread sacking and brought stones for the tracks to grip on, but it ground them under the mud and spat them out at the back, hitting Mark with glancing shots and making him curse me, the allotment and anything else he could think of. When finally it climbed out of the bog, the tractor spattered him with mud and set him off cursing again.

Nearing the far wall at the top of the allotment, I stopped to climb over for the usual purpose of privacy, scrutinizing the area first for any sign of life such as a distant shepherd or horseman. I was convinced that I'd been alone until, climbing back over I paused, as my eye caught a movement about fifty yards away where some large clumps of heather were shuffling along. I hadn't seen the soldiers in training, and with some embarrassment I jumped down to return to my tractor.

Days were shortening now and it was dark as I walked back along the road. Some nights were pitch black when there was no moon or stars. Sometimes it was eerie, as clumps of grass and brambles quivered with small animals moving along the hedgerow. There was frequent scurrying in the ditch and I got a shock when a barn owl glided past in front of me. One particularly dark and still night, a sheep coughed behind a dry-stone wall. Now that is a very human sound and the episode with the soldiers had unnerved me. I stopped with my heart thumping, afraid of what could happen next. Where previously I'd felt comfortable with the dale and the people I knew and could handle, there was a new dimension now, an intrusion.

The days were bitterly cold and I was disking the moor whilst a North East wind blew dark clouds across the sky. It was cold too, crouched behind a dry-stone wall eating my sandwich, from where I could see in the distance, a misty curtain of rain. On the moor beyond the allotment I could see sheep making their way downhill, seeking out any shelter they could find. I stood up and beat my arms about me to generate warmth. Now at the onset of winter the moor was a different place from what it was in the summer. It had been a good summer, a time of trial, but with good laughter.

I remembered the argument when Mark and Eddy were teasing me until the whole thing got nasty and out of hand. We yelled and shouted at each other, but I was so aware that I could not compete in a slanging match that I picked up a handful of soggy earth and threw it just as Mark opened his big mouth. Splat, it went right in, he coughed, spluttered, spat and ran down to the stream to wash it out. He was disgruntled, but Eddy laughed and it settled the argument, so once again we were the best of friends.

As I started the tractor, I remembered the time I chased Mark with the bulldozer. He was quite frightened and told me afterwards never to do that again. I'd known he was quite safe though, I'd come a long way since the Boss said my plowing was like "dog's piss in't snaw," and could maneuver the tractor as if it was part of me.

Just as I was thinking of them, I saw them coming to repair the boundary walls. As I was driving up to the top wall, I could see they were interested in something on the other side. They motioned to me to join them. "Hast thou ever seen a black cock?" Mark asked with a grin, whilst Eddy sputtered with laughter. We all put our heads over to look, and just over the other side, proudly stood a beautiful black grouse, a truly spectacular sight.

Chapter twenty-three

Winter Woes.

Often during the colder evenings, we girls would go to the little village picture house. There we had warmth, rest and relaxation. It wasn't very grand, just looked like an old tin barn, but we enjoyed the jolly atmosphere and the old films that were shown.

The proprietor was a young man, who liked to sit in the back row with his arm round a pretty girl. It all seemed very innocent, just a comfortable way of viewing the film for the umpteenth time and any girl would do, as long as she was pretty. He was also the usher and cashier and when the film snapped; to boos, cheers and laughter, he would disappear into the projection room to help the projectionist.

Sewing was another occupation for dark evenings, as our underwear was wearing out. We couldn't replace it as we were not being issued with any clothing coupons, but we could buy second hand uniform blouses, which we made into vests and panties as they were made from Aertex material. These were probably handed in by girls who had left to get married, or had joined H.M. Forces for an easier life! There was no such luxury as a sewing machine, so we sat around the stoves and sewed by hand.

We would also stop off at a market on our way home some Saturdays, in the hope of buying some parachute material. It wasn't easy to get, but if we were lucky we could use it to sew finer garments, and it was very good for making petticoats.

The handful of us who sewed together had been in the hostel from its opening. We must have been a particularly suited type of individual, capable of enduring the harsh working conditions, the cold and loneliness; and of enjoying the challenge of difficult and unusual jobs. Above all, we were country lovers, not that I heard anyone ever enthuse over the countryside, for when we were not laughing and making the best of things, we were like the farmers, and grumbled.

During the long winter walks to the allotment and back, I was sometimes lucky enough to get a lift from one of the Boss's lorry drivers, taking the timber lorries to and from the forests he'd acquired.

They were big, tough, friendly men, who enjoyed a gossip to relieve the tedium of long journeys. They told me how the Boss would walk through a forest looking at the trees, come out at the other end and give a true valuation of it. The vendor would get his surveyors in, only to find when they'd done their calculations, that their figures would be no different from the Boss's instant evaluation. An amazing feat for a man who had no schooling, who signed his checks with a cross until his wife taught him to read and write. They said one of his latest acquisitions was a forest on a near perpendicular slope, where two tractors would be needed to haul the logs out. One would stay at the top of the bank to assist the other by winch, as it dragged the logs up. They also told me the Boss was rumored to be negotiating a deal for a castle; its land and forestry in the North of Scotland.

I also heard about their mates, about the pubs they went to, their landlords and landladies and the good humored scandal about the driver who had a woman at almost every place he visited, which was known to everyone but his wife. These lifts gave me a good cheerful start to the day's work, better than toiling up the bank in the cold gray chill of a morning, when frosty mists were not yet clearing from the moor.

Lime spreading was one of my jobs, so I had to help load the bags onto the trailer. Our hands and feet were frozen and the only way to keep warm was to work at the double. No need for the Boss to spy on us now, he knew that the only way to keep warm on an open moor was to be very active. I had noticed him in the summer, checking up on me from a distance, so I was grateful to the old countryman who'd taught me how to use my eyes.

Mark and Eddy were working hard and I tried to keep up with them. The bags were heavy and cumbersome and in my haste I dropped one too quickly onto the trailer and it burst. I got a puff of lime cloud in the face; my eyes were stinging badly and were too clogged for tears to wash it away. All I could do was stumble across the rough tussocks to a little stream that cut its way through the peat, and plunge my face into its icy water. My eyes stung all day; and as I couldn't see properly I finished work early to go to the chemist for medication, but they stayed sore for several days.

The final job was mole draining. A pointed cylinder was slipped into the ground and pulled through by the tractor, leaving an underground tunnel for drainage. The weather was wintry, so I often had to brush snow off the tractor seat before sitting down. One of our girls, a county tractor driver, had seen the doctor about her piles and was told to keep warm and never sit on anything cold. Good advice, but next day she still had to scrape the ice off her seat before she started work.

With the mole draining completed I had to drive the tractor back to home farm. This proved to be a nightmare journey as the road and its several bends were steep and shiny so the tracks couldn't grip the surface. It slithered about, gaining momentum as it rushed crazily downhill. I looked down at the valley running parallel to the road, but the view that I'd so often admired turned me cold, as I thought the machine would skid over the edge and somersault to the bottom. I had visions of other dangerous times, when Mark yelled "she's gonna coup," but this situation was more frightening as neither brakes nor gears had much control over her. But with my head buzzing with the noise and rattle of the machine, we hit the level village road and I was thankful there had been no other traffic.

Chapter twenty-four

Pork.

Down at Jack's allotment, the potatoes were being lifted and there were rows of healthy vegetables to feed them through the winter. He'd had his pig killed by the butcher and his wife and older daughters were busy cutting and curing, making sausages and brawn. Nothing was wasted, "not even the squeak," as Jack said. Fat was rendered down to lard and the sides of bacon and ham were hung, providing meat to accompany the vegetables for the festive season and the hard months of the coming year. I was given a parcel of fat, sausages and brawn to take home to my mother one weekend, a wonderful gift in those frugal days.

When I made my usual call to Jack's place one Sunday night, I was given a plate of home killed pork sausages to eat. Whilst we ate, the family watched me, waiting for exclamations of delight. I tried to not disappoint them, but I was not used to rich food and these were so rich and succulent that I found it hard to swallow them. I tried to laugh and chatter as usual as we sat round the fire, but I was desperately trying to quell the queasiness of my stomach. Making an excuse that I had things to do, I left early, hoping that this time Jack's wife would stay with her family. But no, she put her hat and coat on as usual and accompanied me all the way to the hostel, where I dashed in and was horribly sick.

It was evidently the pig-killing season, for there were sides of bacon and ham hanging from ceiling hooks at the farm. There was also a lingering smell of the ham and eggs cooked for the Boss's breakfast. An egg that hadn't been cooked to perfection was floating on the pigswill, which would have been a week's ration back home.

There were several jobs to be done; and 'Old Bill' the only man who wore riding breeches for work, kept me busy. His collie dog kept a safe distance from him, it was not a happy, confident dog, but slunk rather than walked and was suspicious of kindness, a thing it had never known from its master. I surreptitiously tried to be friendly with it, but it snarled at me. Old Bill saw; and told me that a working dog wouldn't work if it was patted or well fed, so I had to abandon my good intentions and leave the poor skinny thing to its misery.

The Boss came back to the farm in his Rolls and called me over. "Gan ower to South allotment and count them Galloways for me," he said. That was the first ground I'd reclaimed and there was now a sparse crop of grass on the poor soil. A few days previously, when the Boss had spoken of his intention to graze the Galloways up there, Mark had protested, "There's nae meat for them up yon," "No," said the Boss, "but they've got a bloody good view."

So once again I was toiling uphill, I seemed destined to six mile round trip hikes, on top of a day's strenuous work. It was an invigorating, gusty day, birds tacking like sailing ships in the wind, bare branched trees guarding distant farms, it was biting cold but I sweated with the climb and the buffeting wind.

There was peace in the lee of the conifers, but little peace in the thought of counting a moving pack of Galloways. I counted several times, then decided on the number as one hundred and twenty. Back down the valley I went and reported the number to the Boss, which he accepted in silence. I thought this was unusual for him and wondered what he'd made of the number, whether he thought he'd gained or lost some. Anyway, this became a daily hike for some time, whatever the weather I toiled up that hill to count the moving herd. Though I counted different numbers each time, I always reported one hundred and twenty, for consistency and I never found out why he wanted to know each day.

My dinners at the farm sustained me through my varying jobs and I enjoyed the company of the young people there. The daughter's boy friend was often there; and the fiancé of one of the sons. She told the

Boss that she'd seen Mark with a girl, to which he replied, "Courting is a young man's job."

Another letter came from Bob, he had seven days leave. This time the Boss was not so willing, but I packed my bags and went anyway.

Jack's wife told me that the men were not happy about me getting so much leave, one week a year was the holiday allowance. I did not care, my conscience was clear for I worked as hard as any of them and it was war work, not a job for life and unlike them, I'd given up home comforts to be there.

Chapter twenty-five

In the Forest.

When I reported for work again, I was told to go to the sawmill, from where I'd travel with my bulldozer, which had been put on a low loader, to a remote forest in the North of Northumberland. My job there was to make a gradual track for the horses to bring the timber down, as the country was rugged and the hill too steep for the men and horses to steady the timber on its downward journey. We left our valley on a cold, dark, winter morning and headed north. I was pleased to see that Mark had been sent along to explain the job and help unload the tractor down its planks.

It was a wild and bleak place; the lower slope had been churned into a morass of mud by horses' hooves around rough stumps and roots. High above were stately pines from whence came the sound of clanging chains and men's gruff voices. A lorry driver had told me once that the Boss employed a lot of ex-criminals as cheap labor so I felt slightly apprehensive of this new situation. Mark quickly took his leave and returned with the low loader.

Now I was on my own. Looking around I could see no screen for a toilet, or shelter for eating my bait. The angle of the muddy hill looked dangerously steep, so I set off on foot to assess the situation. I did not like it, there was barely enough room to maneuver between the tree stumps and if the track was made up and down the hill it would be too steep for holding the timber steady. I'd have to make a transverse route with wide hairpin bends, where it would be difficult to hold the tractor sideways on a hill so steep.

My tractor was cold and difficult to start, my leg was aching before it cranked into life. We started on the lower edge, where in spite of the difficulties I managed to make an impression before it was time to make the journey back to the farm at dusk, on a timber lorry that had just been loaded.

I'd been told that my lifts would be with a respectable man who would also teach me to drive. When I mentioned that I had no license, the Boss said it did not matter, so next morning I climbed into the cab of the timber lorry and with a few instructions we set off through the village and up the hill out of the valley before daylight.

Some two and a half hours later, we arrived at the forestry site, the strain of driving had left me slightly tired and my tractor was in a sullen mood, cold and uncooperative. It slithered in the mud and as I had to work a little further up the hill that day, it had an uncomfortable tilt to it.

The forestry workers on the higher slopes carried on working as if I did not exist, whilst down below, the others who were loading timber onto the lorry using sheer legs and horses, also ignored me. I ate my meager bait while sitting on the tractor; and gratefully drank the hot tea from my flask.

Dusk brought me my transport home and once again I had to drive. My instructor may have been respectable, but I felt he was a man full of resentments and a mean, crusty character. I would have felt more at ease with one of the more jovial drivers.

A few mornings later he said I ought to know the route by now and not keep asking him which road to take. It was difficult as there were neither sign posts, nor place names and no maps allowed because of the war. When I grated the gears he was terse and grumpy and asked in a vulgar way, if I needed the toilet.

That day I had to work even higher up the hill and could look down on diminutive fields and hedges, or across to the rounded hills of the border country, like inverted pudding basins. I could see sleet in the distance and had time to put my oilskin cape on before it reached me. There was mud everywhere, which the slithering tracks spewed up without finding anything to grip. The whole machine started sliding downhill; I was used to it skidding, but not at this crazy angle. There was great danger of it 'couping' and I contemplated jumping. I scanned the slope for tree stumps, as to hit one broadside would definitely turn us over. If my seat hadn't had a small side to it I'd have slipped off and under the tracks. Our desperate journey continued, till at last the lower track gripped something solid and I was able to swing her nose slightly downhill so we slithered at a more reasonable angle to the path below, which I'd just completed the previous day.

Each day took me further up the hill and nearer to where the men were working. When my tractor stopped, I could hear the shout of 'timber' followed by the crash of a falling tree. Men with axes lopped off the branches, then looped chains around it ready for the horses to drag to the stockpile that awaited the completion of the track I was working on. Another two men were busy on the standing trees, with a hand held cross cut saw. They cut into the tree until it could be pushed against the 'V' shape that had been axed out of the other side, then the warning of "timber" filled the air.

They lit a fire at lunchtime; and being numb with cold, I carried my bait over to join them. I sat on a log, one or two of them said 'Aye,' and got on with their bait. I got a few shifty looks; they were a scruffy, mud-caked lot, unshaven and uncouth. The dirtiest most evil looking character shot a spittle of tobacco into the fire. He had mean little eyes in a dirty, puffy face, with tobacco stains in his stubble and dribbles slavered all the way down his clothing. I never heard the other men address him, but when he spoke it was in a Scottish accent that was unintelligible to me.

Driving home at night I felt a relaxed lethargy brought on by the warmth of the cab and the steady drone of the engine, which was not conducive to good driving, or good temper on the part of my instructor. He changed his tune next morning though, when we were driving through a small country town and a policeman was directing traffic at the crossroads. "Carry on, look straight ahead and look as if you've been doing it for years," he said.

My task was almost finished and I was not sorry, twice I'd almost lost a track and just managed to save it from twisting off. Now I understood how the horses had broken tempers from working in the forests if all the men were like the ones I had met, shouting, cursing and lashing them. I had had enough of looking down from a precipitous height, numb with cold, often wet and, with the men and horses already using the track, I thought tomorrow could be the last day.

In fact I never saw the completion of that job, as I fell victim to the influenza that was going through the hostel. The village doctor was called and examined me at arm's length. He was a snob, who treated the girls as if he would catch the smell of a cow byre if he came too near.

Lying in my bunk, I thought of my dear doctor at home, a kindly sympathetic man. When ringworm had been virulent in the summer, the girls who reported to the village doctor had been given a purple tincture to paint on; it neither did any good, nor prevented it spreading. When I noticed I had it, I waited a few days till I could go home and see my own doctor. He was very interested; and while he explained to me that we got it from contact with cattle, he looked through his medical books and prescribed an ointment, which his dispenser made up for me. Within a few days I was completely cured; and there was sufficient left to cure all the girls in the hostel.

I lay with my thoughts; it was a pity that I didn't have the satisfaction of finishing the Northumberland job, in spite of all the dangerous and frightening moments. Now in retrospect, I could appreciate the scenery, especially the time I saw the pale winter rainbow adding a little color to the bleak wintry landscape.

My evening meal was brought to me by one of the wardens, there'd be no pudding for me she said, 'feed a cold and starve a fever,' was her motto. I wondered how I could keep my strength up to fight an infection, if I was hungry and unhappy. Fortunately one of my friends came to take my tray away and I asked her about the pudding. It was ginger pudding with custard, such a treat. She was sympathetic to my pleas and smuggled a delicious bowl to me. Feeling much better, I slipped into a natural, healing sleep.

Chapter twenty-six

Cute Little Lambs.

Some days later, I struggled through deep snow to Home Farm. My bulldozer awaited me and we cleared the snow from the lonnen and the paths leading to the fields where the livestock were waiting to be fed. This was a really easy job on level ground, such as I had not experienced before.

With the snow cleared, I helped with feeding the stock and renewed my acquaintance with the fat old sow. Her last litter had been sold, except for three which were being kept for Home Farm use. The Missus also kept me busy, clothes were washed by possing them in a tub; and I had to do the heavy possing, mangling and hanging out. I enjoyed the latter job, as the clothes-lines were stretched over a small triangular paddock with lovely views over the snow covered valley, where warm smoke curled up from the chimneys. "Stoking up for the dinner," Mark used to say when we were threshing for neighboring farmers, as he kept an eye on the chimneys, knowing it was tradition to give a good dinner to the men who helped out.

All the heavier chores were passed to me; butter churning, cheese making and carrying the whey to the bull calves. A sister who often helped at the house whispered that the Missus wasn't well; she had 'woman's trouble'. This pattern of working between the farm, the house and snow clearing, extended over several weeks. It could have been quite pleasant, except for the Missus's sharp manner and her wanting everything done at the double.

Eventually, pale sunshine melted the snow and warmed the valley. A young American officer and his wife called at the farm one day and he very politely asked the Boss's permission to take his wife to see the "cute little lambs, aren't they so sweet?" The Boss chuckled and brandished his horsewhip, "Aye, tek her along; and mind you shut the bloody gate," he said. Before they were out of earshot the Boss was parading up and down, mimicking them with great affectation, "cute little lambs, well yer bugger, aren't they just sweet? Bloody lambs!" he guffawed. Built like a rotund bull, he was quite a sight as he strode up and down cracking his whip. When the young couple returned with fulsome thanks, the Boss said, "Aye, bring her along any time," and winked at me, "half a dozen bairns she wants." Cracking his whip, he strode off chuckling merrily.

Stones had to be cleared from an inner field, ready for disking, harrowing and sowing. A lethargy I had not felt before overcame me, my legs were heavy as I plodded across the soil to deposit my burden by the hedge. Wild garlic was growing in profusion down by the river and its pleasant clean scent was soothing, as was the song of the birds perched in the branches, proclaiming their territory. Fresh spring leaves were emerging from the hawthorn bushes and I could hear the swollen river coursing merrily along. Later on in the summer, we girls would be bathing in the pool just up river from where I was working.

Our Boss was going to plant potatoes in the field I was clearing; and up on the North allotment, Jack was sowing turnip seed on land near the farmhouse and grass seed on the rest of the reclaimed area.

As I wearily gathered more stones, I thought of the previous night at the hostel. There were a number of new faces there, girls who seemed to have more vitality than us older ones. They chattered about boys and their blistered hands, whilst we were writing letters to faithful loved ones and remaking second hand shirts into vests and panties. I thought of the day I slipped on the ice in the lonnen and hurt my elbow. When I reported for work I fainted; and the Missus just said 'now whatever made you do that?' She asked in the same conciliatory tone that she had on the day I threw a bucket of water at Mark, after he'd thrown one at me, but he dodged it and it went through the open back door. Several times I passed a tree stump, until looking at its large and inviting surface I touched it and found it was warm. I thought I'd just curl up and rest on it for a few minutes. Some two hours later I sat up, shocked to have slept so soundly for so long. Who, I wondered, had seen me? I had lived in the country long enough to know that nothing goes unnoticed, so I rapidly cleared more stones and nonchalantly presented myself at the house for tea time chores. Everything seemed normal; and not a word was said.

Chapter twenty-seven

In the Quarry.

It was said that the Boss never rejected a new challenge and could do every job he expected his workers to do. He seemed to enjoy presenting me with new challenges too. I was driven in the firms' small red van to a quarry, where I had to take the bearing off the stone. That meant pushing away all the soil and growth, to leave the bare stone for the quarrymen to blast. It was quite a large quarry and the men looked at me with friendly interest as I arrived. The foreman came over and told me where to start and what he wanted doing. Sometimes I had to work the bulldozer dangerously near the edge, but the trickiest job was when I was working in a waterlogged section with water coming halfway up the tracks. The ground was very uneven and I couldn't see what I was doing, or where I was going. I had to depend on the feel of the blade, when it jarred I knew I was down to the rock.

Lunchtime in the cabin was quite pleasant, the men were a decent lot and amiable to work with. When the siren blew, everyone had to take cover, but it was difficult to hear over the roar of the tractor. One day when I was concentrating on the job, I neither heard the siren, nor noticed the men disappearing. I just happened to look around and saw the foreman waving and gesticulating frantically, miming that I should run. I stopped the tractor, lowered the blade and jumped out to take cover behind a large rock. As I dived behind it, lumps of stone passed over my head and either side, landing just behind me. It had been a particularly big blast. The men were worried and thought a better warning system was necessary, so they decided that in future they would run a flag up in a prominent position for me to see.

My driving lessons continued en route to the quarry in the little red van. This time I had a nice middle aged man for an instructor and I enjoyed them. The steering was so light compared to the long and heavy timber lorries that I almost put us in a ditch at first. Driving in daylight was strange too, I'd been used to dark roads and reassuring headlights, but my instructor was very understanding so I soon adapted and enjoyed driving along the leafy lanes. My instructor was pleased with me and when my job at the quarry finished he said it was a pity, as I could easily have passed my test after another week's instruction.

It was the same van that Mark had borrowed last autumn when we went to the big agricultural show on Newcastle Town Moor. He, Eddy and I had set off in high spirits and enjoyed all the usual attractions of the show. It was well attended and as Mark looked round the sea of faces, many of them middle aged or elderly, he asked, "when you look at all the older women, don't you wonder where all the bonny young lasses went?"

In the early evening, Mark said he would take us to a Newcastle restaurant for a meal and he selected a really posh one. On entering, a waiter hurried over to us and looking us up and down he enquired of Mark, "Have you sufficient means to cover the cost of the meal sir?" Mark pulled a thick roll of bank notes out of his pocket and showed them to the now astonished waiter, who had no choice but to reluctantly show us to a table. A few well dressed patrons glanced in our direction; and then ignored us, to continue their meal with even straighter backs and more elaborate manners, to further illustrate their social status. Their reactions would no doubt have been different had they known Mark had been to an expensive school and his father was reputed to be a millionaire.

We ordered chicken and when a knife and fork could get no more off the bone, Mark said, "Pick it up in your fingers and waste nowt," so we did, laughing, chatting and enjoying it.

Chapter twenty-eight

Life in the Farmhouse.

North allotment had been planted with turnips and now the rows needed hoeing. A group of us was sent there to do the job under the supervision of the man who lived in the farmhouse. It was not a pleasant job, the repetitive motion of pushing weeds and thinnings from one side to the other, was tiring and boring, especially as it went on for hour after hour. The man in charge set a cracking pace that we all had to keep up with. A little Italian prisoner of war, who sang the classical songs of his homeland, offered light relief. He had an exceptionally good voice, and his songs merged with the beauty of the surroundings, wafting on the sweet clear air.

We chatted to him as we ate our sandwiches, he seemed to have plenty to eat and would smile saying "molto da mangiare." War and the circumstances of his capture, were never discussed, but he was happy to be in England. He enjoyed farm work and the country; and said his camp was good.

All was sweetness until the day when he, Mark, Eddy and I were working together near the farmhouse. Our little prisoner of war walked a short distance away from us, turned his back and urinated. Mark was highly indignant; Eddy saw the funny side but was slightly shocked, they both reprimanded him for doing such a thing in the presence of a woman. Our P.O.W. was quite surprised, he could see no harm in it, as evidently it was acceptable behavior in his country. He made his excuses in broken English and with such expressive gestures that we had to laugh. Equanimity returned, we all got on with the job in hand and his lovely tenor voice was soon in full song again.

Spring was giving way to summer when I was bidden to help in the house, as the Missus was having her operation. Reluctantly I left my beloved fields and fells, the trees were in full leaf and wild flowers crowded the hedgerows as I walked to Home Farm. Fortunately it was quite a modern house with large windows; and I needed not feel too shut in with the back door always open, but I still yearned for the open country.

Soon I was too busy to think, for with the house to tidy, a sink full of dishes, the swill pail to take to the pigs, eggs to gather, the dairy to clean, I found I was working at the double. Neither the Boss nor the Missus had realized that I could not cook and now it was too late!

There was meat for the oven and the gardener came to ask what vegetables I required, there was only one thing to do, emulate what I'd seen the Missus do. I ordered vegetables and stoked up the fire in the range to heat the oven, sweating with heat and panic, I peeled, washed and chopped, filling the big cast iron pans ready for putting on the fire. With the meat sizzling in the oven, I was just feeling a little more relaxed when the Boss came in demanding tea and I had to make room for the kettle amongst the pans. As the time ticked away, I saw that the gravy had not browned and there was no gravy salt in the house. The Missus thought only inferior cooks needed it, as she could produce rich brown gravy without its convenient coloring. Luckily I remembered that one day when her gravy hadn't come up to her usual standard, I'd seen her throw a handful of sugar onto a hot oven tray to caramelize, before stirring it into the gravy to darken it.

As they all trooped in at twelve noon, I began serving the dinner. It was eaten slowly and in silence, all the usual lively chatter was defunct. Then the Boss asked with slow resignation, "Did tha mother never teach thou to cook?" Except for the days the Missus's sister came to help, they had no option but to make the best of my offerings. At least I doubted after that experience, that the Boss would ever again reject an egg fried by his Missus, where the yolk was not dead center and standing proud with an even circle of white around it.

There was never a shortage of anything at the house, for the Boss had plenty to barter with when he wanted wines, spirits or any hard to come by commodity. One day the farmyard seemed unusually quiet except for the chauffeur polishing the Rolls. Old Bill and the Boss seemed wary and alert and there was an atmosphere of anticipation about the place. I was going across to the dairy, when the chauffeur sent me back, telling me to leave it until later. Puzzled, I knew something was afoot, I also heard a van in the lonnen, but it had not come into the yard to turn round. A few minutes later I heard a pig squeal, so putting two and two together I realized that the van had been the butcher's; and that an extra animal or two above the quota had been slaughtered. Now I knew why there was no shortage of meat on the farm and why the Boss could be seen putting well wrapped parcels into the boot of his Rolls. I guessed that most of the dale's farmers would somehow be involved in this bartering system.

It was not long before the Missus was back home, so we put a bed in the downstairs parlor, where it would be easier to look after her. She never complained; the dales people were as tough as the little Galloway ponies that roamed the fells. Their motto was "thou hast to get on with it." She had no comment or criticism of the domestic situation while she was away, her only remark being "did your mother never teach you to cook?"

The Missus asked me to go upstairs to change their big double bed and clean the bedroom. "Shake all the blankets and bedding out of the window and throw the mats out of the window too. Then come downstairs to shake them and put them on the line for a good airing," she instructed me.

I went upstairs, opened the window wide, whipped off the eiderdown and shook it out of the window in one smooth motion. I could not believe my eyes as pieces of paper were floating down like large snowflakes; and glancing back at the bed I saw it was covered with five pound notes. Nobody could have dashed down those stairs quicker than I did, then out into the yard where I picked up five pound notes, chaseing those blown by a mischievous breeze. Gathering my bundle tightly to me I went, rather sheepishly to explain my misdemeanor to the Missus. She was quite unperturbed, "That's where the Boss must have hidden the money," she said, and asked if I'd got it all.

Feeling slightly dazed I went back upstairs, re-made the bed, placing the five-pound notes in neat piles on the bedspread, then carefully covered them with the eiderdown. When the episode was related to the Boss he asked if I'd counted them; and if they were all there. Unsure of his insinuation I told him that every fiver I had found had been put back in place; adding with some asperity, "I might be poor but I'm honest." He laughed, tapped his leg with his horsewhip and quipped, "If you are poor and honest, then you will always be poor."

Life was never dull at the house, apart from the Boss's quick changing moods and the coming and goings of young people with all their laughter; there were also violent summer storms to contend with that year.

Dark clouds threatened our dale, as thunder reverberated around the hills. During one violent storm the Missus carried on with her work as usual whilst I continued washing dishes in the kitchen sink. The lightning was vivid against the black sky and simultaneous with the crash of thunder. The Missus was nearing the open door between the living room and the kitchen, when a white flash came from the radio. It went in a straight line through the open door, missed us by inches and disappeared through the opposite wall. It all happened with such amazing speed that it was over before anyone could feel any shock or reaction. "Does your mother turn the electricity off in a storm?" asked the Missus. "Yes," I replied. "Then you had better go and turn the generator off," she said. I dashed through the drenching rain with thunder and lightning all around me, a fifty yard sprint, then down the steps to the concrete bunker where the generator was housed, turned the wheel that shut the electricity off and sprinted back through the rain to the kitchen.

Though the storm played round and round the valley all afternoon, we had to turn the generator on later, for the milking. I set the table for tea, laying the knives and forks in their places. The storm was right overhead when the Boss and Mark came in. As the thunder crashed, we watched lightning jump from knife to fork all around the table. Nobody commented on the spectacle, but the Missus calmly announced that as I had said my mother turned the electricity off in a storm, I had better run and turn the generator off again. That impassive little woman would rather implicate my mother and me, than give the appearance of being either cautious or nervous.

The Missus was a competent home manager; her house was run smoothly and efficiently. Meals were served on time; and there was a plentiful supply of clean clothes and darned socks. Furniture was polished until it shone and I was even told to polish the wooden feet that supported the sofa. When I washed the kitchen floor I was told I was not doing it the right way, so I was instructed accordingly. "Wet it thoroughly, just a small patch, not too big. Plenty of soap on your scrubbing brush and give it a good hard scrub. Then get your floor cloth and wipe it away, rinse with more water, wring the cloth then dry it thoroughly before moving on to the next patch." She watched me a while then asked, "Did you wash the floor at home for your mother?" "No she had a woman to do the work," I replied.

There was quite a bit of excitement when the Boss came home. He had bought a castle, lands and forest in the far North of Scotland, so they had much to talk about. He was in a jocular mood, riding high on his success and prosperity. "I will take you up there to see it," he told her, "and we will stay in the best hotel in the district." But our Missus would have none of that, "What do I want with a posh hotel," she said, "if I go, we will stay in a caravan."

It was also rumored that he was buying a big hall and estate further up the dale; and there were often business men around the farm, One particular day, the Missus had asked me to clean the windows. I had carried the stepladders round to the front of the house, rinsed my wash leather and climbed up to clean the top of the window, when I heard voices. Our boss was showing a professional looking gentleman around the garden. As he approached me, the Boss gave a great guffaw of a laugh and flicked his horsewhip across my bottom, shouting "and this is wor bloody land lass." It hurt; and I clung to the ladder and yelled "oh yer bugger!" This had the Boss convulsed with mirth, but needless to say, the gentleman looked aghast, embarrassed and not at all amused, which is just the shocking effect the Boss had hoped for.

Chapter twenty-nine

Herding Cattle.

Soon the Missus was quite well again and I returned to the land. Mark, Eddy and I were sent up to the North allotment to bring down the herd of cattle that were grazing there; and put them on the afternoon cattle trucks.

Once again I found myself on my beloved uplands, chasing uncooperative animals. We each had a stick to brandish at them while attempting to turn them in the direction they had to go. It was difficult keeping them in a group with such a wide area for them to break loose and gallop around. We ran for over an hour, shouting warnings and instructions to each other, till I wondered where the cattle got all their energy from.

Eventually we managed to guide them down the hill, past the fenced off land where the turnips were growing and up the incline to the road. As I ran as fast as I could towards the gate, some of the beast tried to break away, "hurry" shouted Mark, "run." "Louse yer trailer and be sharp," Eddy added. Breathlessly I flung the gate open and went into the road to take up a position for turning them. I thought I'd let my rude colleagues herd and guide them through, whilst I stood there panting for breath.

Our journey wasn't too difficult after that, until we reached the village, where suddenly there was temptation up every side road, with succulent plants to be sampled in gardens, much to the annoyance of their owners. It was also time for the school to come out, adding children, dogs and traffic to contend with.

At last we got them over the bridge and along the path to the station. There the stationmaster and the village policeman were waiting to supervise the job of herding the cattle safely into the trucks. They looked cool and calm, in contrast to our disheveled, foot sore and sweaty appearance. We must have looked a very sorry and exhausted sight.

Chapter thirty

The New Estate.

Now that the war was nearing its end, romance was in the air. Flora, the Boss's daughter, was embroidering a fire screen; and I was given materials to make one too. I was accepted as one of the family now and invited to sit by the fire in the evenings, to do my embroidery. We compared our design and colors as we sat chatting, my design was of a peacock perched on a bough of pink blossom. The Missus was usually there, possibly with one of her sons and a girlfriend to add to the company.

Back at the hostel we were embroidering tray cloths and tablecloths, whilst discussing our futures. There was little we could buy for our bottom drawers, for everything was in short supply. One girl heard that utility sheets could be bought at a small town market, so when Saturday came, a group of us went there by bus and bought a pair of sheets each from our meager savings.

Mary asked if we'd like to see the church where she would be getting married, so we all went by bus to her hometown. It was a large church, and very interesting with beautiful statues and lovely stained glass windows. We were walking up the aisle behind Mary, when she suddenly stopped to curtsey to a statue of Our Lady. Taken unawares, we all tripped over her in a heap, scattering our parcels as we fell. Giggling and embarrassed, we quietly retraced our steps and hurried out into the street, where we caught our buses home for the rest of the weekend.

All the rumors turned out to be true, the Boss had bought the large estate up the valley, so Mark, Eddy and I were dispatched to do several jobs there. Some trees had to be sawn down, their roots bulldozed out and the soil leveled. We took turns with the cross cut saw and the lopping off of branches; and used sheer legs to load the logs onto lorries. Architects and builders were busy at the big house, as many improvements were in progress. There were lovely old stables and outbuildings, some in disrepair, so the three of us were moving old scrap metal and the rubbish accumulated from years of neglect. We also worked in the fields and repaired fences.

The house was approached by a long tree lined drive, its entrance guarded by a beautiful lodge, which the Missus looked forward to occupying when the big house was eventually handed over to Mark. In front of the house was the parkland, with a wide expanse of grass dotted by lovely old trees, stretching down to the river.

Back at the Home Farm one day, the Missus was speaking of their plans. The Boss would have highland cattle roaming in the park; and she would have a swivel summerhouse in the garden and peacocks strutting around.

She was also thinking out loud about her family too. Flora and her fiancé were planning their wedding, her eldest son was already married and another two were courting, so she'd thought Mark could have me. It was just slipped quietly into the conversation, but I ignored it and continued with my work. The days of arranged marriages were over.

There had been celebrations when peace was declared, bonfires were lit and a dance held in the village hall. Peace did not make much difference to the farmers, for the majority of them war had meant subsidies and a better standard of living, only a few had parted with loved ones.

For the Land Girls, peace meant a new and different life. A few would marry local boys and settle in the dale, others would marry their fiancés from the forces, but some had no option but to return to the dreary life of shop, office or factory work.

Chapter thirty-one

Time to leave.

Bob and I had got engaged during his June leave; and now as the trees were draping themselves in autumn colors and the hedges were red berried, there came the letter planning our wedding for his October leave in 1945.

I told the Boss of our plans; and that I would be putting in my notice. "Thou disna have to go," he said, and his offer gave me something to think about. Bob would have to return to the army after our honeymoon in Keswick and it would be February '46 before he was finally de-mobbed. Yet I knew I had to make a complete break, like all the girls who had stayed with the hard life for a considerable time, I was physically and mentally weary. We had endured six long years of war and separation, with long gaps between the censored letters and very few leaves in which to meet.

Hostel life was closing down and the girls were packing their suitcases. I would wait at home until Bob was de-mobbed and could come back to me.

I completed my last Saturday morning at work, the Boss and his Missus gave me a beautiful hand cut crystal salad bowl with servers and an inscribed serviette ring. The Boss also gave me a large, white £5 note. Flora gave me a hand cut crystal marmalade jar.

Jack and his wife gave me a blanket, which would have cost them dear from their modest wage; and we promised to keep in touch. We did, they visited us and we visited them until Jack's wife died, forty five years later. But I knew that the family at the farm would remember and talk of me for a while, then forget me as they adapted to their new life at the Hall.

My father and I carried my belongings to the little station, where not very long ago, Mark, Eddy and I had herded the cattle into trucks. We caught the afternoon train, it slipped out of the station, past the sawmill and stables where Helen and I had spent our first few weeks of a cold winter and past Jack's house where I'd enjoyed such homely hospitality.

All that had become so familiar was slipping away, as the hills gave way to flat fields. I said my silent farewells to the heather moors, the curlews, the lapwings and the gulls that followed my plow. Farewell to the steep roads and magnificent views leading to the two allotments I'd reclaimed. North allotment was to become a viable farm, but no other man's investment could give him true ownership. As I had made it with my sweat and hard work, I felt that piece of land would always be mine.

I would also miss my beloved tractor, in spite of the difficulties cranking it into life and the dangerous times when it had skidded and almost couped. Memories would stay with me, memories of clean fresh air and the girls in the hostel, the Young Farmers club, the animals I'd worked with, especially that old sow I was particularly fond of.

Bob too, was giving up the opportunity of a life at sea, working on a trawler. He had always wanted a sea faring career, but been denied it because of the mass unemployment of the 1930s. The war had given him the opportunity of joining the D.E.M.S. (Defense Equipment Merchant Ships) and he had served on trawlers, tankers and general cargo ships.

Our train was nearing the station from where we would catch the final connection for home. At last I knew there'd be no more sad partings on station platforms, not knowing when, or if, we would ever meet again. That was all behind us now, war had brought some adventures, but also a lot of heartache, fortunately we were among the lucky ones who had survived it.

A joyful confidence surged through me as I walked along the platform with my father. Bob and I had no money or home, but we had each other, so could look forward to our future, as our future was together. No matter what difficulties lay ahead, we would share them and see them through.

Our new life was beginning.

PART TWO; BOB'S STORY, THE GUNNER.

Chapter one

The Call to Arms.

Walking along the cliffs, following the narrow coastal path that tracked the edge of a deep inlet, I paused to look down into the bay. This was Manhaven as I'd so often seen it before, with the tide half way up the pebbly beach. In earlier years I'd have been down there clambering over rocks, exploring caves and rock pools, like the youngsters I could see now. They were doing exactly the same things as so many generations of boys before them, totally engrossed in their games and activities.

My thoughts descended quickly to the sandy cove below, where past summer days had mingled with the sand, yet sailed away with the tide. Days when life seemed timeless and imagination could reach to reckless heights, pursuing boyish dreams of bravery and daring as part of the delight of a day's adventure.

Old memories came to play around the water's edge as I watched, of small driftwood boats launched to round the point of the next bay. Excited dreams of success as we sent our boats out on the tide, some with a simple mast, others more elaborate with two or three masts and proper sails. I remembered the cave that could only be reached at low tide, with its secret exit further up the cliffs, which we'd hidden by closing it with a large rock. We could keep a small fire going as long as we wished, make 'tinkers tea' in an old brown can and share whatever we'd brought to eat for the day. I suddenly realised I was looking back over fifty years, to what seemed a significant point from which to recount the many things that would happen in the near future.

I was a young man when the war began, so naturally I was soon involved in the military call-up that presaged the declaration of war on the 3rd of September 1939.

I had already enlisted in the local territorial regiment in the previous year, as events with Neville Chamberlain and Hitler were taking shape, so on Friday the 1st of September, I was mobilised along with every other territorial and reservist.

It began for me in the drill hall of the 296 Battery, 74th Field Regiment, Royal Artillery. Gunner R. Orwin 899227, and what a lucky number that proved to be over the next six years of active service. A group of us had enlisted at the same time, Tom Hastie, Walter Crane, Charlie Young, Bill Matthews and I. The whole battery was assembled in the drill hall, every man dressed in uniform and pack, each with a personal kit bag at his feet on the floor. There were several ranks of men lined up in this order receiving their instructions, whilst others were moving up the hall to the medical inspection area for a basic physical examination. Once this was completed, we were issued with two blankets and told to join members of our troop for billeting instructions. As well as the large drill hall, some Church halls had been taken over at short notice, so by the end of the day over 300 men had been allocated accommodation. Even after we'd settled on the floor to sleep after 'lights out,' there was still a trickle of latecomers joining us. Next morning the hall had been furnished with several ranks of trestle tables and wooden forms. The cooks had been called very early and the whole regiment was provided with a breakfast of tea, bread and sausage, which was our first meal since the previous afternoon. The cooks were not professionals, so the meal was basic, but quickly devoured with great enthusiasm.

We had a few weeks of training while we got into shape, physical exercises down at the beach, military exercises and machine gun training here, on these cliff tops. We gradually improved our fitness; and learned a routine that prepared us for future events.

In November 1939 we moved down to North Leach in Gloucestershire where we were billeted in old barns, farm buildings and a disused brewery. The dining facility was in the Village Hall, right in the centre of the main street. There was a beautiful old Church, a transport café and two pubs. The largest and best Hotel had been taken over by the officers, so was 'out of bounds' to the other ranks, but the smaller pub was better suited to our needs anyway; it was noisy, crowded and merry. You could get a glass of cider for three pence; and three glasses were quite enough to make me happy. Again we settled down to our new routine of daily exercising and drill, with occasional night exercises as relief from boredom.

December 1939 was a bitterly cold month in North Leach, with icy roads and almost continuous frost throughout the days. The guns, tractors and lorries, trucks and some private cars were all parked on a large area of flat ground, ready for moving at any time. There was no anti-freeze liquid available,so all the engines were drained each night against freezing and replenished next morning. The engines also had to be rotated by the starting handle and warmed, every two hours to prevent seizure.

In the fields, blades of grass were finger thick with clear ice that crunched like glass under our feet. Each cold dank morning we slithered down icy stone steps to the ablution shed, which had neither lighting nor heating, where we coaxed a drip of water from frozen taps for washing and shaving by the light of a half candle, which was cherished as a vital piece of personal equipment.

So began a normal day; and when the call came for breakfast we mustered in ranks along the road, with steel plate and bowl clenched in icy cold hands as we marched along to the dining hall. Sometimes there'd be a loud clatter as some prankster knocked his neighbour's plate or bowl from his grip.

The hall was gloriously lit with bright shiny light and a semblance of warmth, to welcome us to breakfast and another day.

It was still not daylight when we returned to the billet, where each man folded his blankets and set out his kit on the bed; his spare boots polished and displayed with soles uppermost to show off the bright studs in proper formation. The billet was left tidy and clean when we were marched off to first parade and inspection, usually at 09:00hrs.

Each man was personally scrutinised for polished brass cap badge, belt and boots and a close examination in full daylight to ensure that the razor had passed smoothly over his face. After this we were inspected from the rear, where nothing could be concealed from Officers or NCOs who were all agreed that hair length on your neck could never be too short, so that a soldier could never be complacent, even though he attended a barber twice a week! On this subject they were so rigid and uncompromising they could reduce an ordinary man to the semblance of an idiot if they so wished.

Chapter two

France and the Evacuation from Dunkirk.

In January, which was another icy cold month, we went with the main guns of the regiment to Salisbury Plain, where we had divisional battle training and regular firing for several days. After living in the snow and ice, we were very glad to return to North Leach and the comparative shelter of our billet with one hot stove in the centre of the floor, which provided our main comfort.

Later that month, our regiment said 'Goodbye' to North Leach. Very early on a cold wintry morning while it was still very dark, we marched through the village for our last meal in the dining hall. Naturally at this early hour no one felt buoyant or full of fun. We quietly took our places at the serving tables where usually you'd get a mug of tea and something on your plate, but on this momentous day all the cooks and helpers had unfortunately overslept following the previous evening's celebrations. They were immediately put on a charge for failing to perform their duties, but the problem then was, who would replace them and provide our urgently needed breakfast? There must have been some feverish negotiations, as eventually the cooks agreed to do breakfast if they were promised leniency for their misconduct. They provided us with hot tea, bread and cheese, which was all we had until we arrived in France at Cherbourg some thirty-six hours later.

There was a sequel to this sad tale that arose once we'd become established in France. Many of our younger soldiers had succumbed to their long period of hunger and against all the rules they had broken open their snow rations of chocolate, which was a grave offence by military standards. This was discovered during a kit inspection and any soldier who had broken the seal on his rations was put on a charge. There were at least eighty of these defaulters in our battery, who every night after normal duties, were marched to the next town and back (St Victeur) for fourteen days. It was about ten miles round-trip, they called themselves the Chocolate Soldiers and composed a suitable song to help them on their way.

From Cherbourg we travelled by train to La Hutte, which was a halt near Le Mans. The train was very basic, shabby and smelly. There were no refinements such as toilets and the regular seats were of slatted wood, very hard and most uncomfortable. There was no upholstery or padding on either seats or partitions, so there was nothing to absorb the noise and vibration that invaded the whole train. When we arrived at our destination, we packed into army lorries which carried us a few more miles to the village of Fiet. Here we dismounted and marched off to our various billets, carrying all we possessed.

Our home was a farm building, which was a byre with a loft upstairs and a layer of fresh straw on both floors. The loft would have been dark without the several gaps in the roof where the pan tiles were missing, but eventually they had to be plugged when heavy snow began to fall, though it still drifted in through any other cracks it could find. No heating or lighting was available, and it was bitterly cold mid-winter weather. We remained here for about four weeks, whilst waiting for our guns and transport to link up with us. The area all around was frozen hard which hampered movement, but eventually they rolled up one day, so at last we became fully mobile as a regiment.

Our next destination was a village called Bouvelles, close to Amiens, where after a few days travel, we were greeted by torrents of rain and acres of mud. Our accommodation was within a huge farmyard with byres, barns and stables on three sides, where we packed into a hayloft with a long ladder for access. Fortunately these billets were dry and weather proof, but at ground level there was no escape from the slushy mud. Even then we were ordered to use dubbin on our boots and were expected to parade daily for morning inspection, clean-shaven, smartly dressed, with boots semi polished and clean. These were high standards for troops that were sleeping on a bed of loose straw; and using cold ablutions and primitive latrines.

There was not much allowance made for the weather or the conditions we lived in.

Our meals hardly ever varied, baked beans, boiled egg or soya link sausages for breakfast, with two thick slices of bread to mop it up. Dinner was always a stew made from fatty beef, carrots and potatoes, covered with a layer of yellow grease and served into your steel mess tin. I believe this must have kept us going during the very cold winter, which we endured mostly out of doors. We ate where we stood, with mud up to our ankles. We often got rice as a sweet, but without sugar or milk, or a heavy suet dough and watery custard, which no doubt provided the sustenance we required. Another bright spot in this very cold existence was that we could walk down to the 'estaminet' at night to fortify our spirits with cognac and rum at very cheap prices.

The local nuns volunteered to launder for us once; and everyone sent in their bundle with names and number for identification. When the washing came back however, it was all loose and loaded on to an army lorry, with no labels to help us identify personal items.

The whole regiment must have exchanged shirts, underwear, socks and towels before it all got sorted out.

The letters from home started to arrive; and we settled into a routine that suited our environment, so the weeks extended into months while we waited for the action to begin.

Training became more realistic and more urgent as the weeks progressed and the weather improved. We learned to move in convoy with each vehicle maintaining its position throughout the exercise. There were also night schemes, driving in total darkness, sometimes with masked headlights or no lights at all. To avoid shunting into the vehicle ahead, all rear axle differentials were painted white, with a small hooded light illuminating it, so nothing could be seen beyond the vehicle following. In spite of these precautions, we inevitably experienced many mishaps that were really part of our individual training.

After some four weeks or so, we moved on to Douvrin, near to Lille, where we were billeted around a farmyard again, in a hayloft with loose straw for bedding.

It must be said that the elements were improving as the weeks rolled on; and at last we enjoyed the luxury of a weekly hot shower in the local colliery baths, which served about forty men, or three lorry loads at one time. You were allowed no more than five minutes to complete your shower, but it was a lovely opportunity to clean up and feel human again. It certainly boosted your morale! Our diet remained almost the same, day after day, but here we could supplement our rations at the local estaminet, where we could go in an evening to order egg and chips with bread, which made a tidy supper.

Whilst we were stationed at Douvrin, the regiment required volunteers to take part in the 50th division boxing tournament held at Loos. Seeing the possibility of a few days away, I came forward with some others to do my bit and in double quick time we were in a lorry heading for the fair. We had been led to believe the next few days would provide us with good food, ample refreshment and a few training sessions to pep us up, but this was cunning propaganda to tempt us into insanity.

When we arrived and dismounted into a large cobbled square, we saw squads of troops doing physical exercises. Some were skipping, some were stretching and others were shadow boxing, they had already been here for at least a few days. We were led into a large gymnasium where we were quickly examined by a doctor, then weighed-in, to be allocated to the division in which we would be matched. We found that the tournament would commence within 2 to 3 hours and that we had only just arrived in time to appear that day! It was a joke to some of us, but others used this as an excuse to back out, which was probably wise in the circumstances. My fight took place in the afternoon, a welterweight bout with a corporal in the RAOC. We were fairly well matched and completed the required three rounds, though we were both equally shattered. Anyhow, my opponent got the decision on points and I retired to get my breathing back to normal, then spent the rest of the day watching the programme, which really suited my idea of sparkling entertainment. We spent the next day watching the elimination contests, then returned to our billets at night, thoroughly satisfied.

Mid May we left Douvrin and moved towards Belgium. We were intending to occupy a section of the Maginot line, but the Germans had begun to move and we were directed into Brussels as a 'flying column' where our stay lasted only a few days. We eventually got into Brussels, having come through Amiens, Arras, Lille and Tournai and we thought we could at last hold some ground here, providing we had some support. Belgium capitulated without warning however, so we had to back pedal quickly, whilst continuing to look for somewhere we could dig in and offer some resistance. Our next position in France was Neuve Chapelle, where we found ourselves occupying a part of the old Hindenburg Line, still prominent after the Great War more than twenty years previous.

Our guns were frequently engaged with the enemy artillery in this sector, where we often took a severe pasting due to the presence of a German Henschel reconnaissance plane that reported every useful detail to the enemy guns. It hovered over our positions, just out of range of small arms fire, where it was a persistent threat to our survival. On each occasion we opened fire, we were quickly pinned down by a salvo of shells which could pin point our position in no time, making things very uncomfortable. Our short bursts of gunfire were in desperate defence rather than attack, as sometimes we were almost encircled by enemy patrols and fast moving columns. Fortunately we could move out at night; and once took shelter in a nearby wood.

After a few more days of this situation our ammunition was running low, so had to be conserved. Eventually we had orders to withdraw, taking us towards Lille. We soon discovered that all traffic was heading in the same direction and the roads were so congested that we were nose to tail and three abreast, moving only a few yards at a time.

Meanwhile ahead of us there were bombers over Lille, circling in the sky then peeling off singly in almost vertical dives to drop their bombs on selected targets. They could rehearse this manoeuvre undisturbed, as there were no opposing aircraft to interrupt the smoothness of their deadly performance.

We were very vulnerable, almost at a standstill with no way of moving in any direction. This was the beginning of the retreat to Dunkirk; and a time when the enemy could hit us from the air without any apparent opposition. And so he did, quite frequently along the journey. We got through Lille after many delays and continued northwards towards the coast. By then we were joined by French and Belgian troops; and a company of Senegalese horse artillery, which added to the increasing throng.

There was also a stream of French civilians fleeing the Germans, who were struggling to make passage in the opposite direction to us. Their column consisted of horse drawn carts, handcarts, pushbikes, loaded prams and people walking with heavy bundles over their shoulders. There were old people, middle aged and younger people, mothers, children and babies, all desperately hungry and weary with a haunted look of terror on their faces. They had already experienced the horror of the bombing and been strafed by machine guns as the enemy pursued them. Many of their lives had already been lost in their bid to escape, how many more would be lost was their constant fear; and the sound of approaching aircraft made them scatter frantically for any refuge they could find. There were farm animals abandoned in the fields, crying out for human attention, which added to the picture of chaos. It was a scene of total desolation and inhumane terror.

We often moved into abandoned accommodation when the roads were becoming impassable, it may have helped to bamboozle the enemy, but we were very often puzzled ourselves about our situation, not knowing of or seeing any constructive organisation to resist their attacks. So we continued to dodge about, whilst our unfriendly aircraft continued to shadow us.

As we moved slowly across France, we met up with other army outfits going in the same direction, so the roads became more congested and chaotic; as more forces were involved. Only in the last few days perhaps, did we hear rumours that the British Army was evacuating from Dunkirk. We could not believe that this was possible, or even practical, but then this was modern war. We had been surrounded, cut off and split up by fast moving columns that had bewildered our generals who had anticipated the old static war that could be played like a game of chess, but this was not going to be like that!

On a final stage of our journey we were about eight miles from Dunkirk. Many of the troops, who had abandoned their lorries, were now marching in single file on either side of the road. All army equipment that was left behind had to be destroyed, so the lorries were run off the road and put out of action in any way possible. By now the congestion had become much greater and at times the traffic moved more slowly even than a tired marching man. Earlier that day, the weather had come to our aid as dark clouds brought a dramatic thunder storm with drenching rain, which grounded the dive bombers that had harassed us along the way.

The scenes of destruction and human suffering were endless; and the drama and tension increased immensely as we entered the outskirts of Dunkirk. Everyone was marching by this time, along a road that was littered with all the debris of war. Our only aim was to march towards the beach, which promised some hope of survival. When the beach and harbour came into view, I could see the whole scene was covered by a heavy cloud of black smoke, rising from the oil installations that had been recently destroyed. It hung over the town and harbour throughout the remaining hours I remember there.

It was Friday the 31st of May 1940. All along the beach from the water line to the sand dunes, there were large groups of soldiers waiting patiently for ships to lift them off the beach. A lot of men had waded into the sea, standing with the water up to their chests, where they waited for small craft to lift them to safety. Unfortunately no place was safe, as many dive bombers continued their bombing and strafing attacks, as well as the low level bombing and heavy artillery which covered the area almost continuously. The air trembled as the Stukas dropped their screaming bombs, whilst the earth shook when they landed. The deafening explosions lifted mountains of sand, which fell like rain as we all hugged the ground. Fortunately the sand absorbed much of the shrapnel and prevented unduly high casualties.

Meanwhile barricades had been hastily erected on the approach roads, which were manned by anybody detailed for rearguard action from any unit that could be brought into use.

There was very little panic and work was still in process immobilising trucks and gun carriers, destroying any equipment that could eventually fall into German hands. Best of all, we were emptying NAAFI trucks of cigarettes, sweets and chocolate bars. These were all we had available to eat and I found a large tin of pears that fitted conveniently into my pack in case of emergency.

I can of course only record my personal experience, as the overall situation was difficult to observe and assess at the time amid the terrific din of bomb blasts that burst right into your ears, to shake your senses and your body.

The Naval Officer in charge of the beach was a remarkably brave man who stood on top of some flat roofed beach huts and spoke calmly through a hand held megaphone whenever he could sense a lull in the bombardment. He could watch the approach of bombers along the beach and shout to us to stay still while the bombs were falling, so preventing a useless human stampede. This he kept up although the explosions were rapidly covering the ground towards him. I believe his name was Commander Marr, I thought he deserved a VC for his actions, as everyone there must have recognised his coolness under such testing conditions.

Somehow I found myself in a bustle of activity where the Red Cross ambulances were discharging their wounded for transferring to the embarkation point. Either I volunteered or someone just told me, but I picked up one end of a stretcher and moved along the beach towards the Mole, about 400yards distant. Halfway along the Mole was a pier or breakwater, where we had to wait until planks and debris were built into a temporary bridge over a bomb crater, but eventually we got alongside a British destroyer, HMS Jaguar and were soon over the rails and onto her deck. The stretcher was taken away from us here, and passed to 'first aid' personnel.

This vessel soon became very overcrowded whilst she was tied up to the quay, then another destroyer, HMS Javelin came alongside and we quickly hustled on board. Once as many men as possible had transferred to this ship, we cast off into the harbour. The air attacks were still continuing and we watched ships sinking and their troops jumping into the sea before they'd even begun their journey home. We hoped they would be picked up and taken on-board some other vessel to continue on their way.

The sky seemed full of dive-bombers like swarms of wasps; and whilst watching some other ships being attacked, I suddenly realised that bombs were falling around my own vessel. It all happened in a melee of bombs, smoke, gunfire and thunderous noise all round. Its nearness only began to register when something swooped over your ship, or whistled past your head, or you felt the heat of a flash like a bolt of lightning. I was standing close to the after end when a bomb exploded and killed the gun crew who were manning the anti-aircraft gun on the poop. We had exchanged words with them just a few minutes previously.

Down below when I escorted a wounded soldier to the sick bay, there was about two feet of water steadily rising. Some of the badly wounded were unable to help themselves. Up on deck there was still quite a lot of action and after one terrible explosion below, there were clouds of steam hissing from the boiler room. Either one or two bombs had penetrated into the engine room so the ship drifted to a standstill, lying sluggishly in the water.

We were wondering what would happen next, when fortunately a small British coaster came alongside where I stood on the port side, so we clambered over the rails and dropped to her deck without wasting any time. She filled up with passengers like the last bus on a Saturday night, we barely had standing room on deck and the holds were full of men gazing up out of the open hatches. We were still aware of the attacking aircraft, but every minute brought us hope as we headed home across the channel. This had been a very busy day, but by nightfall we were headed for Dover.

Though we were all very weary, our nerves were too stimulated to submit to sleep. Most of us had been without real food or rest for days, but what hit us most was the sheer exhaustion suffered from the continuous bombardment on our senses; and the empty hungry feeling of utter despair that haunts a beaten army. We were an unwashed rabble, with fatigue written on our faces, they were very hungry faces too.

By dawn we were slipping into Dover harbour, where the quayside was crowded with soldiers sorting themselves out and marching to the station. I was soon presented with a cup of tea and a sandwich from the WVS, (women's' voluntary service) which was very welcome indeed. Then we boarded a train; and were on our way to an unknown destination. There were several stops during the journey, but eventually we arrived at Devizes in Wiltshire, which was going to be our temporary home. In the station yard we boarded several buses that were waiting; and when I got to the back seat of my bus I found two pork pies that some kind person had left for us. I gave one to my neighbour and we devoured them like wolves.

We got to the barracks and lay on the floor of a hut, with our possessions around us. At least we had got to somewhere we could sleep and eat until we got ourselves back to normal. After seeing the Medical Officer, we were given 48hrs leave and a warrant to travel home. This was about the 6th of June 1940, three weeks before my 21st birthday.

Chapter three

At Sea on a Trawler.

The 74th Field Regiment Royal Artillery was re-formed at Knutsford and eventually despatched to Dorset, where we did further training and guard duties whilst we waited for our guns and equipment to be replaced.

We'd moved to Bridport in Devon, when I had the opportunity to volunteer for a special job outside of the regiment and within an hour I was on my way to pastures new. There had been an urgent call for trained gunners to serve on fishing trawlers, as these ships were becoming popular targets for the Luftwaffe, especially when they had no defence.

I quickly packed my kit, said goodbye to a few of my mates and then I was on my way to Cardiff in an army lorry with 'Ticker' Simpson, who had also volunteered. We reported to a Naval Officer of the DEMS (Defence Equipment Merchant Shipping) in Mountstuart Square, Cardiff, then once on the books we were distributed around the area in various houses. I was lucky, and spent my first few days in the Seaman's Mission, near the docks.

By Monday morning I had been issued with a complete sailor's outfit, oilskins, Sou'wester, sea boots and long stockings, Duffel coat and mitts, one hammock, two blankets, a Lewis gun and cases of ammunition. Then we were taken down to the docks and put on board the trawler 'Iwate.' Our accommodation was in the fo'csle along with the crew; and that's how my seafaring adventures began.

We sailed down the Bristol Channel, passed Lundy Island, crossed the Irish Sea and headed west along the coast of Southern Ireland. Two days of sailing and we were in the Atlantic, 100 miles or so west of Ireland, where we began to fish.

There are no passengers on a trawler, so while we kept watch for any trouble, we also worked, almost around the clock. We hauled in the nets about every four hours and every man was needed on deck then. It took almost two hours to clean the fish and store them in ice down below, after which there was only time for a short nap before you were out again for the next haul. This continued for about ten days until the fish room was stacked full, then we would turn around and go full belt for home.

Once we began to catch fish, they were on the table at every meal from breakfast till supper, with continuous mugs of tea sweetened with condensed milk throughout the day and night. It was a rough life and the trawler never stopped leaning, lurching, rolling and pitching.

From the first trip we had encounters with German planes, fortunately only one at a time. They were Kondors, which would come in at about fifteen feet with every gun blasting at us and a large size bomb to finish us off. While we were firing the Lewis guns, the skipper would be twisting and turning the ship to avoid the bomb, and each time we survived with sometimes only a couple of feet between the bomb and the ship.

I say this truly because you could see the bomb released only a few feet from the ship's side. It must have been frustrating for Jerry, trying to hit a mouse with a sledgehammer.

In our first attack I spotted a large aircraft astern of us flying almost at wave height and circling us for inspection. I hopped onto the fo'csle head where we had a Lewis gun set up on a tripod. I got behind the gun while my mate held the base of the tripod steady against the roll of the trawler. As the plane got directly ahead of us he turned to come in head on at mast height, I waited for his approach, which was very swift. He began to fire his wing mounted canons and as he got nearer I opened fire into the belly of the plane. There was only time to fire one pan at him as he passed overhead so very low and fast, but as he flew away there was a blast of smoke from one engine and he immediately began to gain height as he headed for home. He didn't return, so we were all pleased to have got off so lightly, although the heavy canon fire had extensively damaged our wheelhouse and shattered the instruments and radio in a matter of seconds.

When we returned to Cardiff and reported the situation, there was an inspection by shore personnel who recommended that the wheelhouse should be armour protected, with the gun position moved aft with a thick shield fitted.

The wheelhouse protection consisted of large thick slabs of a plastic type of cement, which were secured to all sides with narrow open slits at head height for observation. It was good protection for the helmsman but we soon discovered that it altered the stability of the ship and resulted in a sudden lurching movement instead of the usual smooth roll from side to side. When she flipped over to her gunwales she filled with seawater that held her until she lurched over to the opposite side. The captain grumbled a bit, but at least it gave better security if another similar attack occurred, the real test would come when high seas and gales hit us.

I spent several months on the Iwate, but I was on my own after the first trip as my mate had gone sick, but not been replaced. We were badly damaged during one attack off Fastnet lighthouse, by a four-engined Kondor that seemed determined to sink us. It expended about six bombs and mountains of canon shell in the process. The outcome was the mate and a deckhand were wounded, and we limped into Castletown, a small harbour in Bantry Bay to put the casualties ashore and recover our senses. We lay for about three days off Castletown; and when we went ashore I had to wear civilian clothing to enjoy Irish hospitality, as it was a neutral country. An Irish gunboat had shadowed us during the attack, but he never took the covers off his guns to give us any support.

After scant repairs we returned to Cardiff for a re-fit, not knowing that the compass and various navigational aids had been upset by the encounter. To make life more difficult we had to find our way through minefields at the entrance to the Bristol Channel.

By the autumn of 1940 I had been transferred to coastal ships; and one of the earliest trips I had was from Falmouth up the West coast past Liverpool to Loch Long, where we spent Christmas awaiting a convoy. Then we went round the North Scottish coast and down the East via Methil, to the Thames. It took quite a time to complete this trip; and I remember passing my home port of South Shields on the midnight watch of New Year's Eve, which was quite frustrating!

I transferred to another coaster in early 1941 and did several coastal trips from the Bristol Channel to Falmouth, Portsmouth and Plymouth; and often through the English Channel to the Thames ports. There were times when it became very hazardous, not with reference to the prevailing weather around the coast, but because of the various forms of action taking place. Apart from the variety of mines, we had 'E' boats (fast torpedo attack boats) and coastal bombers to keep us fully occupied. Around the Goodwin Sands the South East coast was known as 'E boat alley.' Between minefields and sunken vessels, the channel for shipping must have been very narrow indeed and difficult to navigate.

Chapter four

Delivering Coal to Iceland.

I joined a ship called the Hestmanden, (horseman) a Norwegian coal boat which ran up to Iceland to maintain coal dumps where British servicemen required supplies. This meant about six weeks of visiting several Fjords to deliver about 100tons at each point. We met Army and Navy personnel, swapped books and rations, enjoyed horse meat and fresh fish.

We frequently lowered the ship's jolly boat and fished in the fjords. Dusk was the best time to fish and one night we brought over seventy bass on board, which seemed quite a good haul from ordinary hand lines. To tempt halibut we used pieces of fish on a fairly large hook and a much stronger line. We used halyard cord which we tied to the stern sail and lowered it right to the sea bed. Quite often the halibut would weigh ten to twelve pounds, which made a very good meal.

Most places round the fjords were like settlements with only one big general store situated near the quayside, which supplied everything from paraffin to food and clothing, rather like the stores in the American West. We could buy clothing and boots there without having to give clothing coupons. There were also sheepskins and sealskins, which were more of a luxury than a necessity.

I went ashore with the Bo'sun once, to look round a village and meet the people there. He was Norwegian and could quite easily converse with the Icelanders, who were mainly of Danish origin. We were invited into one of their homes for coffee and cake. The room was furnished with a very sturdy table and chairs and a heavy polished sideboard against one wall. It was a fairly dark room with shadowy corners, but almost everything had a knitted cover over it, whilst the remaining furniture was trimmed with a red plush fabric that brightened things up. It reminded me of the old fashioned rooms with low ceilings that were a common feature of farmhouses in our own country one time.

Another feature of the area was that every house around the coast had a large pile of fish bones and offal by the side of the building, which served as their compost heap. To me it smelled like an old kipper factory and I could imagine what it would be like on a warm day. There were cobbled slopes where flat cod corpses were laid out to dry in the sun, which was a long slow process that also added to the atmosphere of the village. These cod, which were as hard as a sheet of thick plywood when thoroughly dried, were a favourite source of nourishment in the winter.

HMS HOOD was sunk in the vicinity of Iceland whilst we were there in October 1941.

When we had finished our deliveries, we loaded sand ballast for the return trip to Scotland. When we got there, we were directed to discharge it in a remote Loch near Rothsay, which took almost a week.

Chapter five

To the Americas.

D uring this period, the Maritime Regiment AA was formed to replace DEMS (Defence Equipment Merchant Ships) and our HQ was moved from Cardiff to the Bristol area, where we occupied a large country house called Kyneton House in Thornbury, Somerset. From here I was re-kitted and despatched to Newport, where my next ship was the Shaw Saville ship Opawo.

I sailed across the Atlantic with her in a convoy to Venezuela, where I left her at Aruba. She was going on to Australia; and as the Japanese hadn't yet joined the war, she didn't need a gunner.

We stayed with a regiment of Camerons who were stationed there, who woke us every morning with the playing of bagpipes. We waited about two weeks for a corvette to pick us up for transfer; and then we embarked for Trinidad via Curacao.

Our billet in Trinidad was an internment camp, where German 'aliens' were detained. It had high wire fencing like a prison camp, flood lights, and observation posts covering the whole camp. It was the only suitable accommodation available.

Trinidad and other British possessions had been leased to the USA in return for shipments of goods to the UK to support the war effort. This transaction had been agreed sometime during 1941, before the Americans became involved in the war with Japan.

We had to slightly rough it for several weeks, providing our own meals from the food that was made available. I mainly remember the fireflies, flying cockroaches, thousands of frogs and the odd snake. Coconut trees, cannonball trees, very strong rum and steel bands added to the variety of impressions.

We were separated of course, from the alien internees, by a road through the camp, with high barrier fences on either side. At night the whole area was floodlit until dawn broke, which attracted bats, mosquitoes and fireflies to the lights. Beyond the perimeter there was a continuous drum like drone in the nearby swamp, from thousands of toads croaking and belching their way through the night. The flying cockroaches were about two inches long; and they lived in the roof rafters, where they constructed honeycomb types of nests similar to a natural beehive. Occasionally you might see a small lizard scampering along the floor, to complete our complement of pets.

We stayed in Trinidad for about four weeks, awaiting transport to the USA. Eventually our ship arrived, a semi passenger Canadian ship called the Lady Nelson, on which we went for a full cruise of the West Indies and a run up to Halifax, Nova Scotia in time for Christmas. We picked up passengers and cargos of bananas and other fruits, along with rum and molasses, bound for Canada.

We were well cared for and enjoyed quite a lot of hospitality from individual crewmembers. They had stacks of rum and cigars that they were taking home for Christmas, though much of these stores did not survive the two weeks it took us to get there. One night after a particularly generous evening of rum drinking, I remember the shock of fresh air when I stumbled out of the cabin, tripping over deck passengers as I swayed back to my bunk. The next few days were uncomfortably hazy, every sip of water seeming to recreate the sense of intoxication. I didn't think I'd ever want to drink rum again after that.

It was intensely cold when we arrived; and we lived ashore in the Seaman's' hostel, whilst we awaited passage back to England. Halifax was a staging post where convoys of ships were assembled for the voyage eastwards to the British Isles. Sometimes it was a fleet of two-dozen ships, or up to forty, depending on the numbers available at the time of sailing. Fortunately we waited only three or four days, then I was drafted onto a Norwegian Oil Tanker bound for the Bristol Channel, along with a gunner from Liverpool.

She was the Pan-Norway and her crew had never been across the Atlantic in wartime.

We carried aviation spirit and petroleum, about fifteen thousand tons of it, which was a large cargo in those days. Nobody liked tankers, but at least we were bound for the UK and not to Archangel in Russia, which was a much harder situation. Russian convoys were notoriously vulnerable to attacks from bombers, air torpedoes, submarines and surface cruisers. Those on Russian convoys had terrible times and temperatures were twenty degrees below zero. Survival time if you ended up in the water was about two minutes.

We got under way just a few days before Christmas and made friends with our Norwegian companions. There were submarines in the area and a Dutch ship that was tail end Charlie was torpedoed and sunk on Christmas Eve. We continued to keep a good look out until we arrived safely in the Bristol Channel, finally dropping anchor off Cardiff on New Year's Eve 1941. The whole ship celebrated in the Captain's saloon with a meal like a banquet, as all provisions had been bought from America where there was no rationing. The lifeboats must have been stuffed with food and spirits, ready for any emergency.

I had a few days leave, then a few weeks ashore back at base, for gunnery training. This brought us up to date with new equipment and tactics and was a chance to meet others who were doing the same sort of job. Though I enjoyed the leave, I wasn't so keen on doing training, though I recognised its necessity. I was always pleased to be on a draft, departing with hammock, kit bag and small pack, to some different seaport where there would be a ship available.

My next ship in 1942 was the Tungsha, which I joined at Newport Monmouthshire. It was another Norwegian vessel, sailing for New York with general cargo.

There was a small cabin for us four gunners, which was merely an upper and lower bunk on either side of a mess table. There wasn't even room for a bench, but the ship had a large galley which provided us with ample food, which was of course our main concern.

There were machine guns on either side of the bridge and a twelve-pound AA gun on the poop, aft. We had a practice fire one day, not realising that this gun was mounted just above the crew's accommodation. The first thunderous crash brought them all up on deck thinking we'd been hit by a bomb.

I got my first view of the Statue of Liberty as we entered New York Bay. The first night I went ashore with another gunner, we didn't have one dollar between us, so it was just a case of looking, but not buying. Fortunately for us gunners we received a dollar and a half for each day we were anchored in New York and the ship's Captain also made some money available to us.

We were loading cargo at the Battery Dockside for several weeks, mainly urgently needed war materials for the services, plus a deck cargo of three large American locomotives and three large tenders. Each one weighed almost a hundred tons and they were held by wire ropes that were welded to the deck. They were of outsize proportions compared to British Locomotives, being twelve to fourteen feet high.

Each time we went ashore in New York it was an amazing experience, as there were so many places to visit. We went to Times Square, Broadway, Rockefeller Centre, 42nd Street Opera House, Madison Square Gardens, Greenwich Village and many of the ethnic districts like the Jewish Quarter, Chinatown, a Russian district and others I can't recall. The 'United States Organisation,' supplied us with top class tickets for any show on Broadway we desired, whilst canteens were open to us for food and drink without charge.

The 'Stage Door' canteen was run by film stars, both the famous and the troopers, where we were made welcome at any time, day or night. I had never experienced such warm-hearted hospitality and understanding. The whole city was lit up at night with neon light advertising, Times Square and Broadway were dazzling and we visited Jack Dempsey's bar. Every place was humming and thronged with people, a vast and vivid contrast to our towns at home that were 'blacked out' in every conceivable way and devoid of any glamour. Our people subsisted on bare rations of food and drink, with no promise of anything but blood, sweat and tears.

Eventually Tungsha was loaded and ready to leave. This was going to be a rough crossing, in mid winter, with westerly winds and high following seas. We sailed on December the 21st 1942, in convoy for the UK. We didn't need Jerry to give us any worries, as we had more than enough already with the top-heavy weight of the locomotives on the deck. Gales blew up, the seas mounted higher and the Captain was anxious about the heavy seas overrunning the ship from astern. We rolled and tossed, wallowed then shuddered up to the surface again until we couldn't hold our position in the convoy.

We found it difficult to sleep off watch, with the constant heaving and rolling. It was hazardous just carrying our meals from the galley, sometimes we'd be walking uphill then suddenly downhill. We rolled with the ship, both hands clutching our food containers to prevent any spillage. We had to hold our plates in balance to eat, quickly scooping up what was possible, when it was possible. The decks were awash with sea water, which didn't help us keep our feet. The whole ship was a clamour of noise and vibration, shuddering and hammering against heavy seas, with every loose object and scupper door adding to the mounting frenzy of wind and sea. The rolling and tossing was weakening the lashings on the heavy locomotives and the decks were buckling under the violent motions of the cargo.

The Captain decided it was imperative that we turned about to face the storm, as there was a risk of capsizing if anything became loose. The convoy left us and we were on our own, with seas forty and fifty foot high running at us like express trains. We 'hove-to' for two days until the wind subsided, then turned about to set a direct course for home, which took about six days. Everyone was on their toes, looking out for any impending danger. Sometime during those days it had been Christmas, but we hoped with any luck, to be on home ground for the New Year. We made it; and we were very thankful when we dropped anchor in Belfast Lough, where we waited to pick up a coastal convoy bound for Liverpool and home.

This brought me to the end of another year, 1942.

Chapter six

Torpedoed.

My mate Jim Waldron and I were despatched to a British tanker berthed near Southampton in January 1943. She was the British Fortitude and she was due for an exciting trip to the United States. We were six gunners altogether on this job, as there were extra guns on board, including a four inch Naval Gun, a twelve-pounder and several machine guns on the bridge. There was no delay in sailing, so off we went one muggy grey morning, into the English Channel where the convoy was assembling. When we eventually got sorted out we made our way heading southwest, so we calculated we'd be taking a southerly route across the Atlantic. We also noted that every vessel in the convoy was a tanker!

We made ourselves familiar with all the guns on board, but without firing any rounds, as we were under the Commodore's control and he would signal when firing practice could take place.

Having six gunners was a treat we hadn't experienced before, which meant the day was divided into three watches. Each watch of two men did four hours on duty, then eight hours off. Up till then I'd been used to doing four on and four off, which was no holiday at all over a long period.

This convoy was special, being all tankers on very urgent business, so a speed of twelve knots had to be maintained, which I think was probably the fastest average speed for any convoy during the war. Anyway, it all happened on the fourth night, about 01:00hrs. I was roused from my bunk by terrific explosions and was soon on deck standing by the four-inch gun on the poop. It was a pitch-dark night and we waited for developments. There were several more explosions in the convoy, when suddenly we got one all to ourselves.

A terrific hammer blow on the starboard side lifted the after end out of the water like a bucking bronco. A tremendous column of water went high over our heads and then descended on us like a wave, completely drenching us, whilst we hung on to rails and ropes. We definitely knew we had been torpedoed. The starboard lifeboats had been shattered, so we directed our attention to the port side ones, in case we had to use them. The ship was still moving fairly fast and nothing could be done until the speed was reduced almost to a stop, so again we were waiting to see what would happen next.

There were seven ships hit that night and I think we were the only lucky one that had not been sunk, despite an enormous great hole in the side which extended below water, almost to the keel. When we realised that the ship was not going to sink, the immediate urgency disappeared. We started to get organised and checked up on various essentials like the guns and ammunition lockers. There was also a welcome rum ration issued to see us through the night. We were approximately a thousand miles out, opposite the Azores when this action occurred, so there were still another two thousand miles to cover before we reached the States.

We duly arrived at Cuba where we anchored in the bay. Divers were sent down to estimate the damage and reported that the hole was something like twenty feet by thirty feet, most of it below the water line. We made it to Florida where we docked at Tampa for repairs and the British Consul there arranged for us to be despatched to New York.

We had a few days to look around at first; and then we loaded our kit onto a Pullman train to travel for almost two days up to New York. We arrived in biting winter frost during February 1943, having just left a sub-tropical climate of about 90°F. We were given accommodation at the Sailors Home in the East end of New York, the Bowery, or skid row as it was called, for drunks and down and outs. This was quite a contrast to our experience of travelling there in 'Pullman' luxury. Soon we were on another two-day train ride, heading northwest to Green Bay,

Wisconsin, north of Chicago. Here we joined another ship, the Laban Howes, which had just been built in one of the Kaiser shipyards, where they could assemble ships in something like six weeks. This was a small vessel however of just about 6,000 tons.

We lived ashore for maybe two weeks until the ship was ready and the crew had been recruited from mainly British 'distressed' seamen, who had lost their ship and were returning to the UK like us. We made our way through The Great Lakes; Michigan, Huron, Erie and Ontario, down to Montreal and the St Lawrence, where we loaded a cargo of Canadian Pine wood. We completed our journey at Blyth, Northumberland, just ten miles from home, so I was able to slip home to South Shields early one Sunday morning and surprise everyone by my unexpected arrival.

We left this ship at Blyth, then travelled down to our base port at Bristol by train, though shortly after, I was travelling back North again for some overdue leave, at home.

Chapter seven

Around the Mediterranean.

During 1943 things had developed in the Middle East following our victories in the desert and the final stages of the North Africa Campaign. I was to be sent there on a ship that was transporting spare munitions from Africa to Italy. We joined the Atle Jarl in Liverpool around June, then soon made a crossing to Belfast where we were provisioned for a long stay in the Mediterranean. For days we seemed to load sides of beef, barrels of salt beef and pork in brine, dried cod as hard as rock and scores of sacks of potatoes and vegetables.

This was a Norwegian ship crewed mainly by Norwegians and a couple of Swedes, plus a Finn, a Latvian, three Irishmen and we six gunners. We had two cabins with six bunks, plus a mess room with a table, benches and cupboards for stores. We ate Norwegian food, which was broadly dried cod, salt beef, salt pork, dried egg and dried fruit. Anything else came out of tins, such as baked beans, meat and vegetables, fish balls and herring, as we didn't have a refrigerator on board.

Early on, I had an encounter with one of the Swedish seamen who I had to chuck out of the galley one night. He threatened me and said I should watch out in future. Late one night however, he was coming aboard drunk and fell between the ship and the quayside. As he had two flagons of ale in his pockets, he never came up again.

The other Swede on board was eventually murdered in a small port in Italy. He had gone ashore on his own and inevitably he had gravitated to a drinking Casa. He was always on his own and quite introspective, but never loud mouthed or obnoxious. He may have got involved in some argument with communists or fascists though and never got back to the ship. He had been stabbed in the groin and was found on the quayside where he had died after crawling his way back a few hundred yards. The Caribinieri came to investigate, but just assumed that his assailant had escaped to Sicily, where he would be well hidden,

This ship was only about three to four thousand ton and our cargo was military and naval stores for the North African Campaign. We soon settled down to the routine of watch keeping, got to know the various members of the crew and eventually arrived at Bone in the Mediterranean, to discharge our cargo. The first thing I began to look for was a mosquito net, which I soon found in the warehouse where we were storing our cargo. I don't know why we hadn't been issued with such an essential item when we given our tropical kit of shorts, vest, shirts and tunics, a sun helmet and khaki socks.

We soon began our programme of operations, sailing almost weekly into North Africa, Italy and Malta, across the Mediterranean to and from ports such as Bone, Bougie, Algiers and Oran. Our mission was to clear all the ammunition dumps from North Africa and transport them to Italy to supply the Italian Campaign. The cargos included shells, bombs, land mines and small arms ammunition. A couple of times we were loaded with aerial bombs from 500lbs each to 10,000lbs. They were all needed to support the advance and we supplied the West coast, the South coast and the East coast alternately, keeping up with the movement of our armies. Twice we took stores to Malta, which had been badly hit and in Sicily we frequently called at Syracuse, Augusta and Catania, where we could always see the familiar sight of Mount Etna, clothed in Ice during the winter season.

Through the Messina Straits we also passed by Stromboli, which was continuously on the boil, with rivers of red hot lava descending down steep sides into the sea, yet people still lived there! Going by the Isle of Capri at the entrance to Naples Bay gave a good view of Vesuvius as we headed to Naples or Torre Annunziata. Our operations up this coast extended up to Livorno in the very north of Italy, whilst on the

East coast we got as far as Rimini. We crept up gradually from Brindisi in the South, through Bari, Barletta and Ancona as the campaign progressed.

We soon got organised in our own way after a few weeks in the Med. We set up a library to exchange books with other ships in the trade; and it was amazing how well this built up from nothing. We also provided ourselves with a surplus of tinned goods, by judicious bartering mixed with a bit of piracy. They included tinned potatoes, which were a special treat, delicious tinned bacon, pilchards, tinned fruit and evaporated milk. These little extras ensured that our diet was adequate for the active, open aired lifestyle that we enjoyed.

When we were in port, alongside, or at anchor, we used to maintain a 'sabotage watch' twenty-four hours per day, looking out for boarders or human torpedoes that could plant explosives on board or under our ship. There were 'frogmen' who would swim underwater to clamp a bomb to a ship's keel.

The Captain was very generous towards us, by offering work in the ship that we could do in our own spare time. I used to keep all the times and dates in a log book documenting the earnings of each gunner, so over the months we built up quite a bit of useful credit. I think we were paid about four Kroner for eight hours.

When we had to take on coal for our bunkers, we would be directed to the coaling vessel, which was usually an old hulk at anchor. We would come alongside to tie up; and then the derricks on the hulk would lower a grab-full of coal into the bunker space. We would be down there dressed only in short pants, to shovel tons of coal into the bunker spaces for storage, working steadily for two or three days. After each shift we would dive over the side and splash about to get rid of the coal dust. We spent a lot of time over the side, swimming about in reasonably warm water. We had no bathroom, only half a salt beef barrel to use as a tub. We got hot water by injecting steam into buckets of cold water until it was really boiling.

Another regular job was painting the hull of the ship. We worked over the side on staging planks, chipping and painting for hours. When we reached the water line, the skipper would 'careen' the ship by flooding one side, which brought her over by about ten degrees, so we could paint each side in turn. The Norwegians are wonderful sailors and seemed to know all the tricks of the trade.

We must have been able to get paint supplies fairly easily, as I think we completely painted the ship about three times.

One windy day I was working over the side, on a plank with my mate Tim. We were chipping rust scabs off with an electric chipping hammer, with pots of red lead paint suspended on lines from the rail to avoid losing them on the rocking plank. We were wearing protective goggles, but their sides were shielded so we couldn't see too well. Unfortunately, while Tim was chipping away, the wind blew a line into the revolving hammer heads, so a pot of red lead was doing circles and splashing paint about like mad. We only realised what was happening when it was so tangled that it reached the hammer, which by then was too late. The chief mate almost had a fit when he saw how the side of the ship had been decorated with splatters of bright red paint.

Sometimes we worked from a small boat, with one line going for'ard and one going aft. This allowed us to pull on one line and give way on the other, to work our way along the water line. It was very dangerous however if you were directly below the garbage chute or toilet outlet; and accidents often occurred.

One late night when I was on sabotage watch in Syracuse, Sicily, I saw the second mate meandering along the dock on his own, trying to make for the ship. I kept a low profile, because he was always stupid when he got full of drink. As he staggered up the rather steep gangway, I suddenly heard him shout as he toppled off into the water. This was a very dangerous situation, as he could be squashed like a lemon if the ship moved. I threw him a lifebelt which he had the sense to hang onto, but as soon as I began to heave on it, the cork it was made of disintegrated into dust and he was left with only a loop of rope in his hands. I got him up onto the quay, then up the gangway and put him to bed in his cabin. He never said thank you, but was very anxious that no one should get to hear about this incident.

This same gentleman nearly shot us all when we were in action one night. We were at the guns in the after gun pit, and he was amidships on a 'monkey island' where we had twin Marlin machine guns with a hair trigger action. He knew little about them and managed to send a stream of bullets over our heads until he got them elevated and pointing in the right direction.

One Christmas we were rather surprised to see the Chief Steward working in the galley, we thought he was doing something special as a treat. Sure enough, he cooked about ten dozen doughnuts, which were exceedingly special compared to our usual fare. Anyway, Christmas Day came; and the Chief Steward went ashore with two suitcases, to visit his Italian friends. He had them filled with doughnuts and we never saw or tasted one. Obviously they were too good for us, or maybe he thought they were too rich for our stomachs.

Sometimes when we were anchored offshore, one of our duties on night watch was to scull a boat ashore, to bring some of the crew back on board. Usually they were very drunk and took a lot of persuading to sit down whilst you did your best to steer them safely back. Sometimes it needed more than one trip to collect them all, then inevitably we'd have to return for some late stragglers, sometimes so many times we became exhausted.

The worst occasions were when they came back in an aggressive mood, looking for trouble. It didn't take much to upset them when they were drunk and depressed.

I remember one night was very spooky. We were tied up at the quay in Catania, Sicily, and the crew had been carousing and meeting up with sailors from other Norwegian vessels. When they came back to the ship the celebrations continued, with singing and shouting into the early hours. Suddenly the noises changed, there began thuds, bangs and angry voices, the prelude to a change in mood. I kept tucked into the shadows, trying to follow events from the various sounds I could hear, because I certainly didn't want to get embroiled in their arguments. Someone had scuppered the party with a tactless remark which escalated in their sensitive state, so old scores had to be settled. The sparks began to fly, next there were shadowy figures quietly moving around the ship and some slipping ashore via the gangway. I remained concealed, but gathered that there were knives out; it looked like a very earnest game of hide and seek.

Though nobody was badly injured, the threatening atmosphere persisted for some time until it eventually got buried in the daily routine of ship work and watches. We had men of all nations and notions, so it was inevitable that the frustrations generated in a confined living space would erupt occasionally, usually fuelled by too much to drink.

Whenever our carpenter came on board at night, he would ask if any strangers had come on board, because someone had threatened to get him. This man was built like a bear and he could pick up a forty-gallon drum of oil by putting his arms around it, and lift it clear of the deck.

The trouble had started when we tied up in Augusta, Sicily. I was on gangway watch to prevent anyone getting on board, when from the after castle there came sounds of uproar, then a Norwegian sailor came lurching towards me with his head split and his white shirt covered in blood to the waist. The carpenter had hit him with a hammer following some disagreement, causing the sailor to go to hospital. His friends from another ship were determined to get revenge and the carpenter was very frightened. He was haunted by fear whenever we came into port and camped out in the paint locker. He eventually left the ship to escape, but before he went he brought all his tools on deck and threw them as far as he could, then tipped his tool chest over the side. He muttered something in Norwegian, walked down the gangway; and was never seen again.

We were short of firemen (boiler stokers) for a while during our travels. We'd had Arab firemen, a Czech who'd been in the Foreign Legion, two Spaniards, an Irishman and now we'd signed on two Italians. These consisted of one big giant fellow and one fairly slightly built. They didn't make much trouble, though the 'big feller' used to pose a lot, standing inches taller than everyone around him.

All went well for a while, then one trip they discovered we were sailing for North Africa, so immediately began packing their cases because Italians were very unpopular in that area following Mussolini's African campaign. When we anchored in Sicily, at Syracuse, to await a convoy, the Italians came up on deck with their cases packed, ready to jump ship, but we had strict orders to keep them under guard in case a fishing boat came alongside to assist them. Meanwhile the Captain went to the bridge and signalled ashore with the Aldis Lamp and very soon there was a motor launch heading towards us.

When it arrived, two British Marines climbed on board and we took them to the skipper's cabin, amidships. After a short discussion the skipper sent for the two firemen, who were now vociferous, excited and hopeful about leaving the ship on the launch. We hustled them into the saloon and I stood watch on the door, where I could see what was happening. The Captain was explaining the situation to the two marines, one of whom; the sergeant, was medium built and leathery looking. The two Italians were shouting, shaking and waving their hands about, with their suitcases by their side, ready to go. This lasted for about ten minutes, with everyone arguing and the sergeant trying hard to pacify them, in his best Italian, but no solution was forthcoming.

In the end he asked the captain if he would leave the matter to himself and the other marine. Left alone with the two soldiers, the Italians erupted again in a volume of abuse. Eventually the sergeant stepped up to the big one and drove his fist right into his mid section. He collapsed like a burst balloon! Immediately the smaller Italian got onto his knees and put up his hands in reverent supplication, utterly shocked that his big mountain friend was stretched out helplessly on the saloon carpet.

They were both escorted back to the crews' quarters aft, along with their suitcases. The marines returned to their launch and back to billets. The captain returned to his saloon; and settled into his chair, thoroughly pleased that the whole event had taken place with such meticulous diplomacy.

Our Irish fireman could be a bit of a handful too, as he was a hopeless alcoholic who spent every penny on drink. He was picked up so many times by the police in North Africa, that we eventually locked him in the calaboose for his own safety. We took his meals in for him, to keep him fed, but he was never appreciative. On board ship he would lower his shoes on a piece of rope over the side, to any boat that would give him a bottle of 'vino' in exchange.

Some of the crew obtained a barrel of vino from a merchant in

Syracuse. It was about a yard across, and four foot long. They shipped it on-board with a winch one night and parked it behind the well-deck staircase. They filled buckets from it and had drinking sessions with other crews.

One dark night, the skipper had watched the cook, fully dressed in 'whites' coming up the stairs with a full bucket, balanced at head height. As he reached the deck level, the skipper neatly tipped the bucket over him by putting his toe underneath and lifting it up. The Captain then ordered the barrel to be removed.

Our Norwegian Bo'sun was missing in one North African port, when the ship was about to leave. He was eventually discovered in some drinking place and was brought back in a 'gari,' a horse drawn cab. He was unconscious and had to be slung on board in a cargo net and put straight into his cabin. He never recovered though and was taken to hospital in the next port, having been poisoned by some local hooch.

We had both the Christmases of 1943 and 1944 on board the Atle Jarl; and I must say that the Norwegians were really sentimental about their celebrations. For Christmas '44, the steward had ordered food supplies from the agent in Algiers. Imagine our surprise when all the meat and poultry was delivered to the ship, still alive. We were creased with laughter watching two Arabs trying to persuade two sheep to come up the steep gangway, while the hens and ducks still in wooden coops on the lorry, were kicking up a tremendous clamour of clucking and quacking. It was natural in hot climates not to kill meat until it was required for eating. Eventually the sheep were sent back to be slaughtered; and we hung the meat up in a cool place behind the bridge, as we didn't have a refrigerator on board. The poultry were killed soon afterwards on the ship and we helped out with the killing and cleaning, to earn an extra pot of jam from the steward.

The celebrations began after lunch on the 24th of December, when bottles of wine and spirits were opened and everyone cleaned up ready to enjoy the day's festivities. There was also a plentiful supply of almonds, dates and oranges, which were easily obtained in North Africa. The Christmas dinner began about 18:30hrs. and everyone was served lavish helpings of soup, fish and poultry. Fruit jelly with cream was served for dessert, as the Norwegians don't have Christmas pudding as we know it. In fact the ships stores had included a number of Christmas puddings, but the cook thought they were cake, so served them cold and uncooked, sliced on a plate.

After the evening dinner, the crew gathered in the skipper's saloon for drinking and toasting, singing carols and some old Norwegian folk songs that brought tears to the eyes of usually very tough sailors. No doubt the Aquavit and whisky were also making everyone sentimental, especially when so far away from their families on such a homely occasion, but what was most impressive was the unusually cordial atmosphere that united men and officers when social barriers were lifted. This was common on other Norwegian ships I served in, but could not have happened on a normal British ship, where the differences were always constantly maintained.

The evening's celebrations were concluded as the bottles became empty, so by midnight the ship and everyone in it were asleep, to dream perhaps of Christmases past and those yet to come when peace would reign.

We often called at Bougie in North Africa, to load ammunition and stores for Italy. The Arabs did all the work manually here, with one gang on the quayside and another on board ship, with some down in the hold to stow the cargo below. There would usually be about a hundred altogether, with a French civilian overseer watching progress. If there was an interval when there were no lorries on the quay for unloading, the Arabs would have a spontaneous break, when they would form half circles and clap and chant endlessly in a slow rhythmic beat. At the centre of this formation, one of the older Arabs would do a slow shuffling dance on the spot, moving his body and hips in time with the rhythm. Steadily the beat became quicker and the chanting and clapping became louder, while the surrounding action became more exciting.

One day the chanting had reached its climax, so the dancing had become really hectic, when the big French overseer jumped up on the ship's rail, dropped his trousers and presented his backside to the crowd, moving it to the rhythm of the dance. Naturally this created a merry riot and the Arabs ashore started pelting the target with stones, mud and anything they could find, until the Frenchman had to retire and make himself decent again. The incident served as entertainment, which certainly kept the Arabs happy and content to go back to work when the lorries started to roll up again.

Another time, we were loading ammunition at Bone in North Africa, and two holds were about half full with various shells, mines and bombs. Ahead of us on the same quay was another ship of about 10,000 tons, which had been loading for days and was nearly completed ready for sailing the next day. As usual there were hundreds of Arabs involved, some working on the ship, some on the quay and some just shouting and adding to the chaos. The gangs on the quay were loading ammunition boxes into cargo nets, which when filled, were swung over the open hatches of the holds, to be lowered down for off-loading and stacking.

I was at the top of the gangway checking everyone that came on board, when I heard terrific yells from the other vessel and saw a cloud of smoke rise from one of her holds. A large shell had slipped through the net and plunged into the hold, so everyone stampeded! They swarmed off the ships, over the sides, down the gangways, slithered down ropes, any method to get off and ashore. The noise and shouting filled the air, as though a flock of gulls had gone berserk. The crowd moved like rapids in the Rockies, with the First Mate in the lead. I stood shocked as hundreds of panic stricken people had pushed and jostled their way past me in the narrow alleyway. I felt like I'd been through a mincer without moving. The humorous aspect of it was that if both ships had exploded it would have been like an atom bomb, flattening everything for miles around, so running away was utterly futile. We learned later that fortunately it was only a smoke bomb that had gone off; and nothing else had detonated.

Chapter eight

At Anchor.

Altogether, we had a varied existence in this area of the war and nothing was certain regarding the next port of call, as orders were often changed to meet the requirements of the day. Our original charter had been for six months, but this was extended so many times we were on this job for almost two years.

We fetched and carried as necessary and seemed to get involved in almost everything that was happening, including taking our explosive cargo to the landings in Southern France in 1944, where we discharged it into landing craft off the coast of Toulon.

This expedition started in the harbour at Oran in North Africa. There was hardly any breeze to cool the still air, as I leaned on the ship's rail, watching the sluggish motion of the sea lapping along the hull plates of the vessel's tall sides. We had just dropped anchor and I'd finished my spell of sabotage watch around the ship, so I was now relaxing and taking in the scene. We had recently received a cargo of ammunition and armaments, and were awaiting orders regarding the next stage of operations.

The hot, still atmosphere around us was much cooler than the sweltering heat we had endured during the days in port and several other ships were anchored nearby, as they too had been loaded and despatched offshore to wait. At least we had company around us, which afforded some little reassurance; and I enjoyed the number of various types of vessels there, which could be observed at leisure.

No seaman can resist the satisfaction of observing another vessel, whether at sea or in port. He notes its appearance, its flag, its bulk and design; and of course he looks for any signs of active life on board, such as another seaman engaged in some familiar task around his ship.

The heat of the afternoon seemed to smother any signs of urgent activity, though occasionally the rattle of an anchor cable could be heard as it tumbled out through the hawser pipe and plunged heavily into the sea. This gathering of ships large and small, was a prelude to the assembling of a large convoy which would head for the southern coast of France, to begin a landing of troops which would move North into action to support the campaign in France which was already underway.

We were observing strict precautions to avoid detection, all vessels 'darkened ship' before dusk, as no lights could be shown that would disclose the position of the ship under cover of darkness. Any garbage that was to be dumped overboard could be an obvious sign to U-boats if it included tins, bottles boxes or any article that could remain afloat and provide a clue that ships were in that area. All tins had to be squashed and flattened and all bottles broken before they were cast overboard, usually during the hours of darkness.

Each vessel carried a large board bearing a three figured number, which indicated its position in the convoy and all the ships' names had been obscured, so we were all in the same state of anonymity for the foreseeable future.

The nearest ship to our starboard side was a Frenchman of moderate tonnage. On her deck was an assortment of small crates containing live poultry, sheep and possibly other livestock that could not easily be seen, but would provide fresh meat and eggs to the crew. I idly watched the activities of a seaman on this vessel, as he set up a table under a white canvas awning, in preparation for an evening meal. This completed, a steward in a white jacket laid the table and set up chairs, then began carrying dishes of fruit and bottles of wine, placing them carefully on what was becoming a well-laden table. Two or three officers waited on deck until eventually the Captain emerged from his cabin and took his place at the table. The officers simultaneously stood by their chairs and at a nod from their superior they assumed their seats.

It seemed amazing to me, to witness such a ritual at this present time, when the main situation was building up to a terrific climax and we were depending on the success of the whole operation. The dark red wine was poured, an ample measure for each man at the table. The Captain raised his glass in a gesture towards his companions; and then turned in my direction and purposely raised his glass again, to include me in his friendly 'Bon appétit'. I waved a hand to acknowledge his indulgence; and felt at once a feeling of pride and of embarrassment, as I had so obviously been watching their ceremonial behaviour.

I quickly left my position at the rail, thinking that very soon I'd be seated at our own mess table, with my friendly shipmates, sharing a humble meal of 'black pan'. This consisted of all the leftovers from the midday meal, fried until it justified its name. This surely serves as an illustration of a seaman's' lot, he is ruled by the man on the bridge, and the ship is his home, indeed his world. Fortune is sometimes kind to him, yet often so cruel, but the sailor can accept both sides, just as he rides the seas whether they are rough or calm.

Chapter nine

De-mob.

In the June of 1945 I'd become engaged to Connie who I'd known for some eighteen months before the war broke out. Though she'd been in a reserved occupation as a telephonist in a shipyard, she'd chosen to join the Land Army. We decided to get married during my next leave, which occurred in October. I had to travel some 300 miles by train to get there and made it just in time. Then after a week's honeymoon in the Lake District I had to return to the army to await my demob.

It was Christmas 1945 and I was at Larkhill, Salisbury Plain. I had been at the school of Royal Artillery doing a surveying course whilst I waited for my 'demob' date. The camp was close to Stonehenge on Salisbury Plain and I had been on this course there for about six months. It was a very large camp, mainly used for training young recruits. When Christmas came, everyone wanted to be home on leave, but some of us had to stay over this period to look after the place, so it was left to a handful of 'veterans' to stay behind and make the best of it. I remember having a whole Nissen hut all to myself.

On Christmas Eve I went to the 'Penny Gaff' which was the slang name for the garrison theatre, where the show was 'Waldini and his Entertainers'. I had seen them previously in Naples and he recited verses about an old pair of shoes that had tramped all over the world. He also had girl singers and dancers, who were very popular with the troops. After the first half hour they decided to stop the show because there were so few spectators. Instead, all the entertainers and audience assembled in the buffet, to enjoy drinks and laughter. We had a spontaneous party, which went on for two or three hours and was a good start for the Christmas festivities.

On Christmas morning my first job was to keep the boiler going for the hot water supply, which was a nice warm job to have during the winter months. After working on the boiler and stoking up in the morning, I enjoyed a leisurely wash and shave, then went along to the cookhouse for breakfast, which was usually two soya links and a ladle of baked beans with bread and butter. Not bad for those days!

I had the morning free and it was a crisp sunny day with air like wine, so I borrowed a messenger's bike and cycled round the local villages, working up an appetite for my Christmas lunch. At Christmas, dinner in the army is in complete contrast to normal. The men take seats at the table whilst the officers serve out the meal. Each man is also entitled to a bottle of beer. The menu consisted of pork with stuffing, mashed potatoes and vegetables with apple sauce. We had Christmas pudding for sweet of course, served with rum sauce, which was a great treat to us in times of so many shortages.

Going back to earlier days before the winter, some of the old hands used to go out in the evening, hunting rabbits. The butchers would pay two shillings and sixpence for each rabbit, which was good money at the time. One night a group of four men went on the Plain, equipped with a bicycle on which they'd mounted a stack of batteries and a powerful spot light. They also had a Lurcher dog to chase the rabbits. They would search out the rabbits in darkness, dazzle them with the light, then quickly dispatch them with pick handles.

They'd had a good haul; and scores of rabbits hung around the bike, but when they decided to make for camp, they found they were enshrouded in a thickening mist. They decided on a direction to take and walked steadily on until they reached the site where an aircraft had crashed. They sat down, had a smoke and rested for a while. After some discussion, they moved off again, feeling wearier, even the dog was limping. The mist became thicker, muffling their lamps ability to probe the darkness. They dropped their rabbits, which were becoming too heavy to carry and tried to find any way of getting off the plain and on to a good road. They eventually discovered another crashed aircraft and decided to rest again, but after a few minutes realised it was the same plane they had visited previously, so they had walked around in a complete circle.

Fortunately the mist was lifting by then and as dawn was gradually breaking, they got their bearings and made for the main road that bordered the plain. They arrived back in their billets just before 'reveille' at 06:30am, footsore and weary, without sleep or rabbits! They had something to be thankful for though, as often there was early morning gunfire practice over the plain, which commenced at dawn.

And so my active service drew to a formal end, I was demobbed and returned to my wife and the buying department of a shipyard on the Tyne. After all our excitement of the previous years, our only wish was to settle down to an ordinary peaceful life. And, I am pleased to say that is how it has been. Despite the usual ups and downs we have been very fortunate. We have our memories; and at the end of the day, life is good.

Lightning Source UK Ltd.
Milton Keynes UK
16 March 2011

169347UK00001B/147/P